"To the immortal name and memory of George Washington"

The United States Army Corps of Engineers and the Construction of the Washington Monument

by

Louis Torres

Historical Division
Office of Administrative Services
Office of the Chief of Engineers

For sale by the Superintendent of Documents, U.S. Government Printing Office
Washington, D.C. 20402

Foreword

At a ceremony on 21 February 1885, President Chester Arthur dedicated the newly completed Washington Monument "to the immortal name and memory of George Washington." A century has since passed, and the white shaft remains the most distinctive feature of the capital skyline.

The monument was many years in the making. Disputes over design, difficulties in raising funds, and the construction itself all added years to the process. The delays ended when a small civilian-military team from the Corps of Engineers, led by Colonel Thomas L. Casey, took over construction management.

The Corps of Engineers had a long association with the monument, during and after construction. Even before the Civil War, Engineer officers provided advice on the soundness and stability of the foundation. Later Casey, who was then officer in charge of public buildings and grounds, took over and saw the monument to completion. Casey's successors managed and maintained the monument for nearly 50 years until establishment of the National Park Service.

This history marks the monument's centennial and pays tribute to the men of the Corps of Engineers who carried out the project, among them Bernard Richardson Green, George W. Davis, and most notably, Thomas L. Casey. This book should be of interest to people associated with the Corps of Engineers or those who are otherwise interested in the history of engineering in the United States.

Paul W. Taylor
Colonel, Corps of Engineers
Chief of Staff

The Author

Louis Torres served as a government historian for 32 years, more than half of them with the National Park Service where he completed several histories leading to the preservation, restoration, and interpretation of national historic sites. He is the author of numerous articles and the book **Tuckahoe Marble: Rise and Fall of an Industry.** He is also co-author of a history of Fort Stanwix, New York, and its role in the American Revolution. Since his retirement from the government, he has been a historical consultant. He completed his graduate work at Columbia University.

Acknowledgements

The author is indebted to the staffs of the National Archives, the Library of Congress, and the University of Colorado Library for leading him through the maze of documents and government publications concerned with the Washington National Monument. He appreciates the constructive criticisms made by Frank N. Schubert and Dale E. Floyd of the Historical Division, Office of the Chief of Engineers, while the study was in production. Finally, a word of thanks must go to Linda W. Greene, who edited the draft, Lael H. Cleys, who typed it, and Constance Potter, who edited the final version. Any errors in this book are entirely the author's responsibility.

Table of Contents

Chapter I.	THE IDEA OF A MONUMENT	1
Chapter II.	THE IDEA BECOMES A REALITY	7
Chapter III.	THE INTERREGNUM	25
Chapter IV.	REVIVAL OF INTEREST	31
Chapter V.	THE MONUMENT RISES	59
Chapter VI.	THE MONUMENT IS COMPLETED	89
Chapter VII.	THE LATER YEARS	99
Notes		115
Bibliography		133
Index		141

General George Washington as Commander-in-Chief of the Continental Army. Painting by Charles Wilson Peale. *Library of Congress.*

Chapter I

THE IDEA OF A MONUMENT

Hostilities in the War of Independence came to a conclusion with the defeat of the British at Yorktown in October 1781 but not until 1783 did the Treaty of Paris officially end the war. The young nation faced numerous problems. The Continental Congress—the only semblance of national unity—had to disband troops and out of an empty treasury had to pay those who remained under arms as well as the domestic and foreign creditors. It had to manage extremely shakey foreign affairs, adjust state boundaries, and deal with jealousies and bitterness among the states.

Despite these serious problems, the American people deeply appreciated their independence, which they sincerely felt they owed to one man—George Washington. Washington had not yet left his country's service for his beloved Mount Vernon when on 6 May 1783, Arthur Lee, delegate to the Congress from Virginia, proposed that an equestrian statue be erected in his honor. Congress immediately appointed Lee, Oliver Ellsworth of Connecticut, and Thomas Mifflin of Pennsylvania, to prepare a plan for such a statue "where Congress shall fix their residence."[1] With surprising speed, the committee reported within two days, but the entire Congress took longer. Undoubtedly it had more pressing matters to consider than a statue, but the delegates' chronic lack of attendance may also have prevented more attention to the plan.

On 7 August 1783, with ten states represented, Congress unanimously passed the committee's report authorizing the erection of an equestrian statue of Washington. The congressional resolution specifically required:

> that the statue be bronze: The General to be represented in a Roman dress, holding a truncheon in his right hand....The statue to be supported by a marble pedestal, on which are to be represented, in basso relievo, the...principal events of the war, in which General Washington commanded in person....[2]

Because America had few artists skilled enough to sculpt such a statue, the resolution directed that a European sculptor under the guidance of the American minister at the Court of Versailles execute the statue and

1

that the United States treasury cover the cost. Congress also directed Charles Thomson, Secretary of Congress, to obtain for the American minister at Versailles the best possible portrait of Washington as well as an accurate description of the events that were to become a part of the base relief.[3]

The 7 August resolution could not have been more specific about congressional plans for a memorial to Washington. The site of the future capital remained unsettled, however, for several more years. Meanwhile, the many problems facing the young nation, particularly with an empty treasury, prevented any further realization of the resolution.

The next several years were critical ones for the United States. The Constitutional Convention met in Philadelphia in 1787, and after extensive deliberations enough states ratified the Constitution to make it effective. Established in 1789 in New York City, a new government, more serious than its predecessor, examined the question of a site for the new capital. In 1790, it selected an area on the Potomac River for the future city of Washington.

Pierre Charles L'Enfant, a sensitive and egotistical Frenchman, but an able engineer, received a commission from General Washington to draw up a plan for the capital. In 1791, he submitted his design, which even included an equestrian statue of the general. He placed the proposed statue approximately where the Washington Monument stands today, noting that this was the memorial that the late Continental Congress authorized in its resolution of 1783.[4] This statue of Washington would be a center of attraction because of its location between the Capitol and the President's mansion.

While Federal City, as Washington, D.C., was then called, was slowly rising, little was done to realize the dream of the old Continental Congress. Indeed, some of the fault lay with George Washington himself, who would not accept the idea of a memorial while he was alive. While Charles Peale and other American artists were busy painting and sculpting busts of Washington, the equestrian statue remained a dream.

In the meantime, Washington served two terms as President and returned to Mount Vernon, where he died in 1799. His death shocked the nation. Perhaps as much from a feeling of guilt because nothing had been done to honor him as from a feeling of adoration, voices rose from every corner praising the lost hero. In Congress, where political parties had yet to develop distinct philosophies, members rose to honor Washington. Among them was John Marshall, then a representative from Virginia but later to become one of the greatest justices of the United States Supreme Court. Following his impassioned speech, the House of Representatives appointed Marshall to a joint committee that was to present a plan showing what "respect ought to be paid to the memory of the man first in war, first in peace, and first in the hearts of his countrymen...." The committee's report, submitted on 24 December 1799, recommended that a marble monument be erected in Washington, and that Washington's family be requested to permit his body to be deposited under it. The report also suggested that "the monument be so designed as to commemorate the great events of his military and political life."[5]

Henry Lee, a fellow Virginian, rose in the House of Representatives to support the resolution. He cautioned his colleagues that Congress should suppress any differences over the design of the monument for the sake of unanimity and action. Anticipating that many quarrels and disagreements would ensue on this issue in the years ahead, he said:

> one hope is cherished, that whatever is done, will be unanimously adopted.... A difference of opinion will naturally prevail. This difference of opinion, however, commendable, upon ascertaining the mode of public mourning; ought to be suppressed when we come to act; for unanimity then is...most to be wished for....[6]

Both houses of Congress approved the resolution on the same day, but problems were about to begin.[7]

The 1799 resolution differed in two major respects from the 1783 proposal. First, it directed that the statue be built inside the Capitol, then under construction, and second, that Washington's body be laid to rest there as well. Although Martha Washington reluctantly agreed to have her husband's remains moved to the Capitol, Congress failed to act. For years afterwards, Congress considered several proposals, but did not enact any legislation because of a depleted treasury, the international situation drawing America closer to war, and disagreements over the design of the monument.

**George Washington in his later years.
Painting by Gilbert Stuart.**
Library of Congress.

On 8 May 1800 Henry Lee offered a proposal supporting the 1783 resolution and stating that the government execute an equestrian statue and place it in the center of a designated area in front of the Capitol. Another House member, Robert Goodloe Harper of South Carolina, moved to amend the resolution by substituting a mausoleum for the statue. The House adopted the latter plan.[8]

The House quickly appointed a committee to study the matter. On the following day it reported a bill that provided that the mausoleum base be 100 feet long and of a proportionate height. Harper, the author of this plan, had asked Benjamin Latrobe, the eminent exponent of Greek revival architecture in Philadelphia, for advice. Latrobe suggested a design of a "pyramid of one hundred feet at the bottom, with nineteen steps, having a chamber thirty feet square, made of granite, to be taken from the Potomac, with a marble...sarcophagus in the centre, and four marble pillars on the outside, besides other proportionate ornaments." He believed that such a design would cost $62,500. In spite of strong opposition to Harper's bill, it passed after a third reading, but Congress did not appropriate any money to carry out the legislation.[9]

At the following session, a group of congressmen led by Henry Lee introduced a similar bill to construct a mausoleum. By now, however, there was some controversy over whether to construct a mausoleum or erect a monument. Heretofore the House had favored a mausoleum, but now some preferred a monument that would commemorate Washington's military and political careers. Much of the discussion centered around expense. To some, even Latrobe's estimate of $62,500 seemed excessive. Congressman John Nicholas, motivated largely by economy, favored a simple, plain monument.[10] Congressman Abraham Nott did not believe that a mass of stones in a mausoleum would add to Washington's reputation or express any more national affection than would a simple marble monument. This being the case, he preferred the latter, which would be less expensive.[11]

When Willis Alston proposed an amendment to build a less expensive monument, Lee declared that the bill should remain unchanged. He maintained that no expense was too much for so great a man. Nathaniel Macon retorted that he favored the amendment because it was more rational and economical and conformed to the intentions of the old Congress. The committee concluded its meeting without reaching a decision.[12]

Many in Congress feared that a mausoleum housing Washington's remains would prove far more costly than originally estimated, perhaps as much as $150,000 or even $200,000. William Claiborne, the group's exponent, suggested that the public would view such an undertaking as a "profuse and useless expenditure of the public money." He felt that principles of economy better justified a statue similar to the one that the Continental Congress originally recommended and that the American people would ultimately support it.[13]

The debate over the type of commemoration continued throughout December 1800 amid bitterness and recrimination. Some members favored a mausoleum, others wanted a monument, and a third group suggested both. Congress also disagreed over the artistic details. Cost was at the heart of much of the argument, although those who urged economy wished to avoid the stigma of being considered too parsimonious in eulogizing so great a man.

The final vote was a close one. The House agreed upon a mausoleum, and on 1 January 1801 passed an appropriation of $200,000 for its erection. The Senate, however, failed to act upon the measure and the issue remained unresolved.[14] Momentous political and diplomatic questions then absorbing the attention of Congress and the country continued unabated until the War of 1812 and made the senators reluctant to vote for a structure that many people considered extremely costly.[15]

The question of erecting a monument or a mausoleum remained dormant for 15 years. On 16 February 1816, Congressman Benjamin Huger, who had served on the 1799 monument committee, rose to ask what could be done to resolve the problem. Congress appointed a joint committee. The committee approved a resolution to build a marble monument "in the centre of the great hall of the Capitol," presumably meaning the rotunda, where Washington's remains would ultimately rest. Congress again failed to pass the resolution.[16] The divergent feelings on the subject had changed little since 1800.

Three years later the Senate revived the question and adopted a resolution to build an equestrian statue of Washington, as proposed in 1783, "in the Capitol square," but it postponed and eventually dropped the matter after the House proposed amendments.[17]

An impassioned speech by the young congressman James Buchanan in January 1824 failed to arouse Congress. The House tabled his resolution but resurrected the one passed in 1799. Years later, after becoming President of the United States, Buchanan reminisced:

> When, thirty-four or thirty-five years ago, I was a member of the House of Representatives, at that time a young man and a new member, I introduced a resolution, the object of which was to redeem the plighted faith of the country to erect a monument to him to whom its warmest gratitude was due. I do not remember at whose instance I did this, but it was undoubtedly at the instance of some respectable citizens of Washington, who remembered the obligations which had been incurred by the previous action of the national legislature. Being then, as I have said, a young man, there was, perhaps, something of the sophomore in my dealings with the subject, but I pressed it with all the ardor of my youth. It was considered at that time, and was so remarked in Congress, that it was rather an indignity that any effort should be made to raise a monument to the

honor and memory of Washington besides that which existed in the hearts of his countrymen. I do not remember what was done, but I do remember the extreme mortification which I suffered from the ill success of the movement.[18]

James Buchanan. *Library of Congress.*

In 1832, the centennial of Washington's birth, Congress appointed a joint committee of both houses to prepare a proposal for a fitting monument. The committee recommended, among other things, that John A. Washington, a descendant of George Washington, agree to move the remains of his illustrious forebear from Mount Vernon for interment in a mausoleum beneath the nation's Capitol, which had been provided with a simple vault. The usual arguments arose, but John Washington ended the debate by refusing to allow the removal of the remains. Once again, Congress failed to memorialize Washington in the manner suggested in 1783 or 1799.[19]

In other lesser respects, however, Congress suceeded. It agreed to commission John Vanderlyn, a well-known artist from New York, to paint a full-length portrait of Washington, which eventually hung in the Hall of Representatives opposite the portrait of Lafayette. Vanderlyn copied the head from Charles Stuart's famous painting of Washington. During that same session, Congress commissioned Horatio Greenough to sculpt a statue partially copied from Houdon's famous bust of Washington. Although Greenough designed the statue for the rotunda, it stood on the east grounds of the Capitol in later years.[20]

The Vanderlyn portrait and the Greenough statue were minor attempts to commemorate Washington during his centennial, but they were not intended to fulfill the resolutions of 1783 or 1799. However, some individuals later argued that the Greenough statue was a sufficient memorial. Congressional attempts to fulfill earlier Washington memorialization pledges occurred later, but the results were feeble and negative. A monument to Washington would have to wait.

Chapter II

THE IDEA BECOMES A REALITY

The Washington National Monument Society

It became apparent that if left to congressional action, a monument to honor Washington would never materialize. Congress was widely criticized for not acting. The prestigious *National Intelligencer,* the leading newspaper in Washington, denounced Congress and the American people for their apathy.[1] Apparently, if any action was to be taken, it would have to be by the private sector. The *National Intelligencer* called for a public meeting of the citizens of Washington to consider the matter and redeem the pledges of Congress. The appeal gained the support of many leading citizens. One such person, George Watterston, a free-lance writer, city alderman, and former Librarian of Congress, concluded that only a direct public appeal would gain the needed results. Watterston became the spirit behind a growing movement to make the long-awaited monument to Washington a reality.[2]

George Watterson.
Library of Congress.

Prompted by Watterston and others, a public meeting convened in the aldermen's chamber of the City Hall on 26 September 1833. The large number of citizens who attended showed considerable interest and earnestness. After reviewing the congressional failure to fulfill promises over the past 30 years, the group concluded that it could not expect that body to be more successful in the future. The group therefore organized the Washington National Monument Society, consisting of citizens largely from the Washington area. Their object was to erect a monument to Washington's memory through voluntary contributions from the general public. The newly formed organization quickly appointed committees to draft a constitution and by-laws, devise a practical plan for raising funds, and prepare an address to the nation.[3]

At its second meeting on October 31, the Society adopted a constitution and by-laws and elected officers. Chief Justice of the Supreme Court John Marshall, who had offered the 1799 resolution in the House of Representatives, became president of the Society. Other elected officers were Judge William Cranch, first vice-president; John P. Van Ness (mayor of Washington), second vice-president; William W. Seaton, third vice-president; Samuel H. Smith, treasurer; and George Watterston, secretary. The Society also elected a 13-member board of managers, one of whom was the historian Peter Force. Meanwhile, the organization established its headquarters and offices in basement rooms of City Hall, where it remained until 1878.[4]

John Marshall.
Library of Congress.

When Marshall died in 1835, 85-year-old former President James Madison succeeded him as president of the Society, although he realized that his role would be honorary. In 1839 the Society amended its constitution to make the President of the United States its *ex officio* president. The first to hold this position was President Andrew Jackson.[5]

The organization carefully selected competent agents to collect funds throughout the United States. In nearly every instance senators, representatives, or other political leaders of a state or territory nominated the agents for appointment by the Society. After appointment, the Society bonded the agents and required them to maintain accurate records of their funds and report at frequent intervals. When the agents forwarded the funds to Washington, the Society's treasurer placed the money in banks. The agents received a commission of 10 percent, later increased to 15 percent, for their services. Of the large number of agents, only two failed to account for the money they collected up to 1855. The Society publicized the fund-raising campaign through the press and the pulpit.[6]

To permit the widest possible participation by the public in the fund raising, the organization limited personal contributions to $1 per year. Within three years, contributions totaled only $20,000. From time to time, various groups raised small contributions at special events, but, in general, the $1 donations kept the campaign alive. Progress in raising funds was slow. The financial problems and the depressed state of the economy in 1837 affected fund raising. The agents suspended collections for several years, despite the Society's urgent appeals for more money. In 1845 the Society wisely removed the $1 limit on contributions, and, for a while, subscriptions increased. The amount raised grew to $62,450, but the Society still had a long way to go.[7]

In addition to removing the ceiling, the Society resorted to other fund-raising devices from time to time. It appealed to school children and women's organizations for money, put contribution boxes in post offices, and asked census takers to hand out subscription blanks. After 1836, each contributor received a souvenir lithograph of the winning design. In the form of certificates, these lithographs bore the autographs of such prominent individuals as Zachary Taylor, James K. Polk, George M. Dallas, Henry Clay, Millard Fillmore, John Quincy Adams, Daniel Webster, and Albert Gallatin. For those contributors who preferred other lithographs, the Society also printed certificates with portraits of Washington. In spite of these efforts, the Society garnered only $87,000 by 1847, a relatively small amount for a 12-year campaign.[8]

Because of its lack of success, the Society inevitably became the object of criticism. Ironically, Congress was one of the Society's principal critics. To allay any possible fears of mismanagement or misuse of funds, the Society decided to place all of its business before the people in a statement to the nation, but the censuring, however unjustified, did not cease.[9]

The Robert Mills Design

To spur enthusiasm and encourage contributions, the Society decided that it must convince the public that the monument eventually

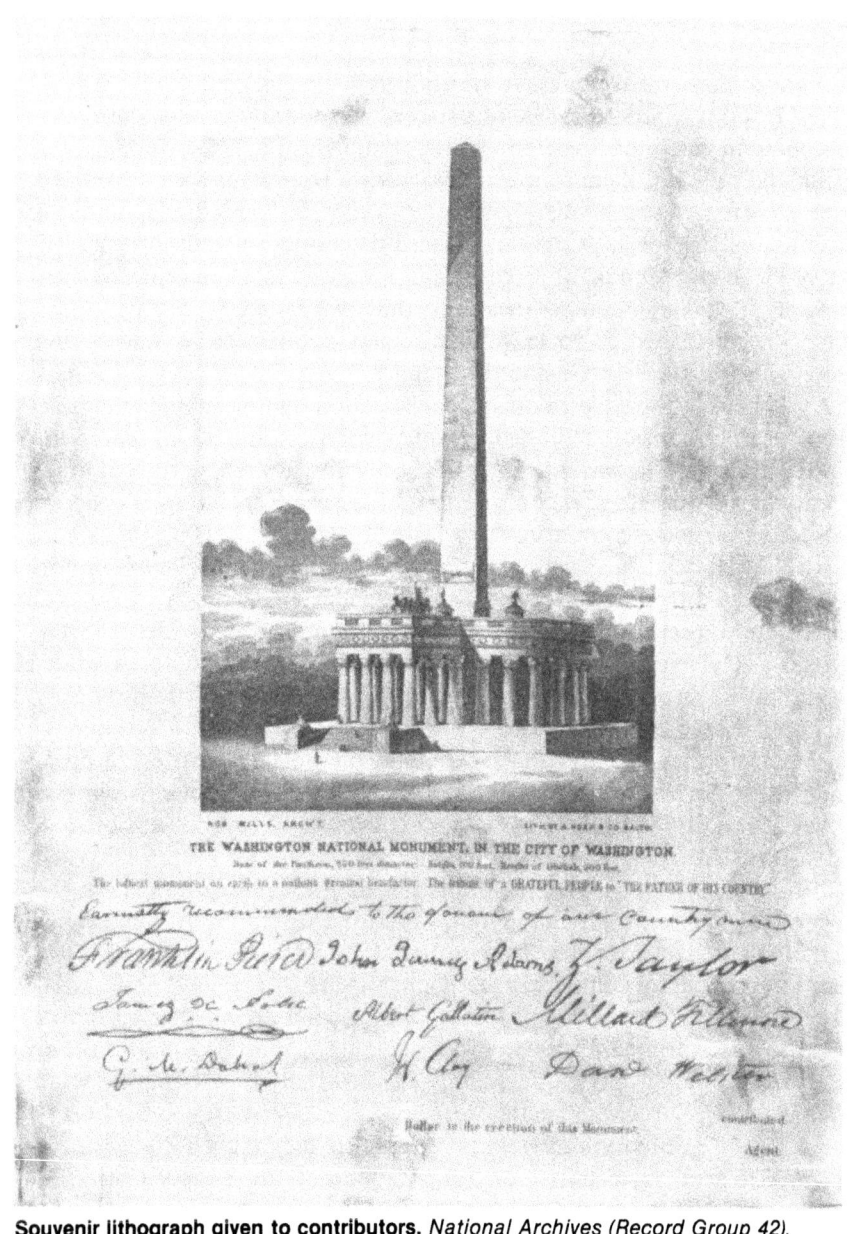

Souvenir lithograph given to contributors. *National Archives (Record Group 42).*

Robert Mills. *Library of Congress.*

would be erected. Therefore, the Society resolved to solicit designs. On 6 July 1836 the board of managers appointed a committee and directed it to prepare a notice for publication inviting designs for a monument costing at least one million dollars. The Society published an advertisement on August 10, requesting designs from American artists and imposing only one limitation—any plan offered should "harmoniously blend durability, simplicity, and grandeur."[10]

The response was excellent. The committee reviewed many designs, including one that resembled France's Arc de Triomphe. After consulting with experienced architects and studying all of the plans, the Society selected one by Robert Mills.

Mills, a former student of Benjamin Latrobe, had designed many Greek revival homes, customs houses, and other federal buildings. Furthermore in 1814 the citizens of Baltimore had selected his design for a monument in their city—the first important public tribute to Washington. For that monument Mills designed a tall Greek column surmounted by a statue sculptured by Causici. In 1836 Mills became Architect of Public Buildings in Washington, a position he held for 15 years. During that period he was chiefly responsible for the designs of the famous Treasury Building, Patent Office, and Post Office.[11]

For the Washington monument in the capital city Mills blended Greek and Egyptian architecture. Monumental in scope, it included a grand circular colonnaded pantheon 250 feet in diameter and 100 feet high. Above the roof of the pantheon, he proposed a huge obelisk.

Mills took great pains to describe the elaborate pantheon. There was no doubt that he intended to give this part of his design considerable emphasis. Meanwhile, he described the much simpler obelisk in these terms:

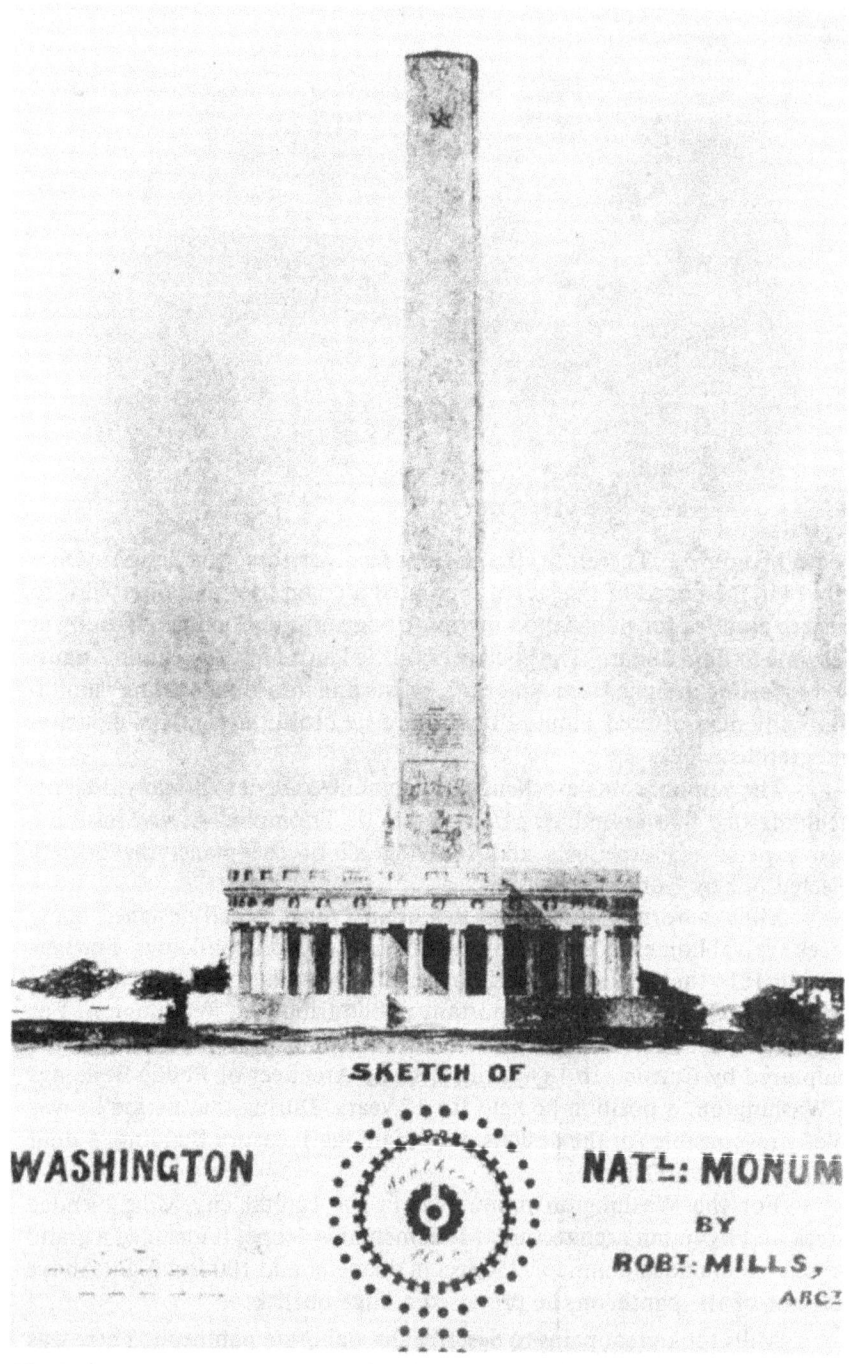

The Mills design. *Library of Congress (photograph USZ62-21953).*

> In the centre of the grand terrace, above described, rises the lofty obelisk shaft of the monument, 70 feet square at the base, and 500 feet high, diminishing as it rises to its apex, where it is forty feet square; at the foot of this shaft, and on each face, project four massive zocles, 25 feet high, supporting so many colossal symbolic tripods of victory, 20 feet high, surmounted by facial columns with their symbols of authority. These zocle faces are embellished with inscriptions, which are continued around the entire base of the shaft, and occupy the surface of that part of the shaft between the tripods. On each face of the shaft above this is sculptured the four leading events in General Washington's eventful career, *in basso relievo,* and above this the shaft is perfectly plain to within 50 feet of its summit, where a simple star is placed, emblematic of the glory which the name of Washington has attained.[12]

To reach the top of the column, Mills planned an easy-graded gallery within the shaft which could "be traversed by a railway, terminating in a circular observatory, 20 feet in diameter, around which at the top is a lookout gallery, which opens a prospect all around the horizon."[13]

Surrounded by 30 columns of massive proportions, the rotunda formed the base of the monument. A 20-foot-high entablature, or upper wall, crowned by a 15-foot-high balustrade, surmounted the rotunda. Mills estimated the cost of the obelisk alone at $552,000, and of the entire monument at $1,222,000.[14]

Mills' design was consistent with the classical tastes of the period. As early as 1813 he had described his philosophy concerning structures of this nature. He believed that solidity, simplicity, and a degree of cheerfulness should characterize all monuments, which should not permit the mind to turn away in "gloom or disgust." A monument, he noted, should "perpetuate the virtues of the deceased" and emanate an "air of cheerful gravity."[15]

Although his design basically followed his philosophy and, in general, conformed to the conditions in the Society's advertisement, simplicity was not one of its major attributes. While the Society favored Mills' plan, professional and artistic circles did not fully accept it. For many years it was the object of scorn, which delayed its implementation. Early critics called it an "ill-assorted blend of Greek, Babylonian, and Egyptian architecture."[16]

No less important an architect and critic than Henry van Brunt claimed that America lacked a sense of education in the arts, a standard of excellence, and professionals qualified to criticize it. Writing in 1880, just before construction of the unfinished monument resumed, van Brunt stated that "no person interested in our reputation as a civilized people can contemplate this completion without pain."[17]

Criticisms of Mills' design continued well into the 20th century. Talbot Hamlin, a student of Greek revival architecture, said that if the original design, which added a tremendous Greek Doric oval pantheon to the simple obelisk, had become a reality, it would undoubtedly "have damaged its absolute and unified perfection."[18]

Doubts and criticisms of the original plan were so widespread and persistent that they ultimately reached Congress and the Society. Some of the objections raised within the Society, however, were due more to the cost than the design. After all, the Society had only raised $31,000 by the end of 1838, far less than the estimated $1 million or more necessary to construct the monument. That same year, George Watterston issued a general statement to the effect that "We have not abandoned the hope that a plan, which at its inception, was hailed with unequivocal approbation, may yet, with proper modification be effected."[19] Apparently Watterston was hinting that even the Society was having second thoughts about Mills' original design.

While Watterston's statement that the Society would not abandon the design was reassuring, several years elapsed before the organization finally made up its mind. In the meantime, one architectural firm that had submitted a design in 1836 noted that although four years had elapsed, they had not received notification of a final decision. Moreover, given the current rate of subscriptions coming in, it would be 50 years before the Society would have enough money. By then, the firm stated, new architectural tastes would render the 1836 designs obsolete.[20] Fortunately, the Society did not have to wait that long.

Meanwhile, the Society received other criticisms and opinions. In 1844 the House Committee on Public Buildings and Grounds entered the controversy, complicating matters even further. In recommending to Congress a site for the monument, the committee concluded that a "temple form" was the best design. The Society would have to build the monument "upon such a scale as to be capable of containing the busts and statues of the Presidents of the United States, and other illustrious men of our country, as well as paintings of all the historical subjects which have or may be designed by our artists through ages yet to come." The committee proposed that the monument be 150 feet high surmounted by a statue of Washington on its dome. On 25 May 1844, the House of Representatives introduced a joint resolution that contained in substance the committee's recommendations. Because Congress would have to pass legislation granting a site for the monument, the Society reluctantly but wisely opposed this design. Congress failed to act on the resolution, and the final question of design as well as the site remained undecided.[21]

A sense of realism and practicality rather than any serious questions about the adequacy of the design led the Society to doubt the Mills proposal. Many felt that with the paucity of funds and the improbability of extensive future contributions, the Society could not build the entire monument that Mills conceived then or later. In early 1848 a committee began considering the pros and cons of the many objections to the Mills design. On 11 April 1848 the Society, acting upon the committee's report, decided to build only the obelisk, fixing its dimensions at 500 feet high, 55 feet square at the base, and 35 feet square at the top. It left open the question of a pantheon, terrace, and landscape. Meanwhile, contributions by now totaled $87,000— enough to begin work.[22]

The Society had not abandoned the idea of a pantheon or an equivalent structure at the base of the monument. In fact, the colorful and elaborate certificates offered to contributors as late as 1848 included two lithographs. One was the original Mills design containing both the obelisk and pantheon with the caption "The Mon[ument] Complete With The Pantheon." The second was a view of the obelisk alone with a plain terrace at the base.[23]

Construction Begins

The Society's announcement of its plans to begin work on the monument forced Congress to decide on a site. Suspicious of the whole project, Congress hesitated to donate a site. The Society chided it for inaction.

Although some in Congress felt that Greenough's statue was sufficient to honor Washington, it received severe criticisms. This adverse attitude spurred the Society to increase its fund-raising activities and push forward its request for a site.

At this time Congress became more concerned with the beautification of the Mall. Previously, appropriations for the city of Washington had been directed primarily toward improving Pennsylvania Avenue and other important areas. The Society, which historically had always favored a site on the Mall, felt that now was the proper time to force the issue and threatened to purchase a site on privately-owned property.[24]

Unwilling to see this happen, Congress acted. Besides, the monument on the Mall seemed to be a good idea. On 31 January 1848 Congress passed a joint resolution that authorized the Society to erect a monument "upon such portion of the public grounds or reservations within the city of Washington, not otherwise occupied, as shall be selected by the President of the United States and the Board of Managers of the Society."[25]

The Society selected a site at public reservation number three on the city's plan. The site contained about 30 acres near the Potomac River, directly west of the Capitol and south of the White House. L'Enfant had chosen almost the exact site for a statue of Washington 56 years earlier. L'Enfant's site had been at the intersection of the city's east-west and north-south axes (the intersection of the White House and Capitol axes). Unquestionably a dramatic site for a monument of this nature, isn't use was ruled out by subsurface conditions and swampy and unstable earth. On 12 April 1848

President Polk executed the deed that transferred the land to the Society.[26] The site was about 370 feet east of the White House axis and 123 feet south of the Capitol axis.[27] This deviation from the L'Enfant plan later caused many problems for landscape architects working on beautifying the Mall. The construction of the Lincoln and Jefferson memorials eventually rectified the lack of symmetry produced by the Washington Monument.

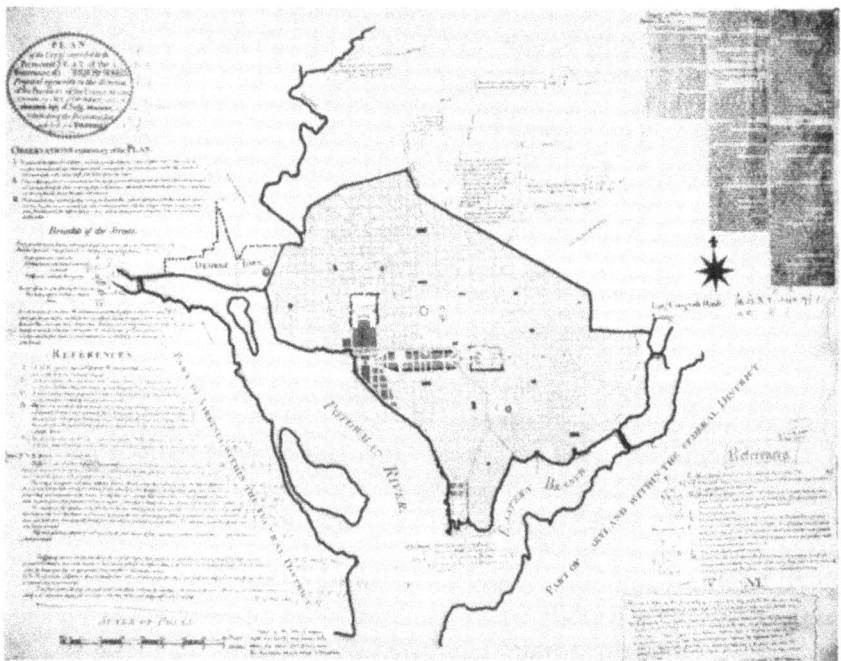

L'Enfant's proposed site for a monument to George Washington is located at the circle where the axes of the White House and the Capitol come together. *Library of Congress (photograph USZ62-8909).*

The monument location remains one of the Society's greatest achievements. In addition to its designation on L'Enfant's plan and the fact that it had President Washington's support, the site possessed a beautiful view of the Potomac and elevated the monument so that it could be seen from all parts of the city and surrounding areas, including Mount Vernon. Also, because it was a public reservation, the government could prohibit the erection of any obstructions. Finally, the site was so close to the river that contractors could easily ship materials—stone, sand, and lime—there at relatively little expense.[28]

After selecting the site, the Society appointed a building committee to administer contracts, make major appointments, and handle accounts—in short, provide general supervision of construction. Almost immediately, the committee constructed temporary facilities at the site to shelter the stonecutters and store the stones shipped to the site. The committee also built a watchman's house, lapidarium, latrines, and other wooden facilities. Also, the committee ordered the erection of rigs for lifting stone, both at the wharf and at the monument site.[29]

To obtain building materials as soon as possible, the committee quickly negotiated contracts for the delivery of gneiss, marble, and blue stone. In 1848 William Early of Washington received a contract to deliver blue stone for the foundation. The blocks were to measure not less than 16 feet long and 7 feet thick. After Early delivered the stone to the wharf adjacent to a road leading up to the site, a rig hoisted it from the scow onto wagons drawn by oxen, which then conveyed it to the site.[30]

Thomas Symington provided the marble for the superstructure from his quarry near Baltimore. The committee thoroughly tested the strength of the marble before signing a contract and found that it could bear a pressure more than 15 times greater than it would normally sustain in any part of the monument.[31]

When the rough marble arrived, stonecutters dressed and polished it, and stonemasons put it into place. At that time, stone-dressing was changing from a slow and tedious manual process to a mechanical one. Many in the industry believed that machinery was more economical and certainly faster than the manual process. Areas such as New York City, where much marble construction was popular due to the rich Westchester County quarries and the interest in Greek revival architecture, already used machinery. William Dougherty, superintendent of construction, who worked under the guidance of Robert Mills, tried to convince the building committee to use machinery by demonstrating that during 1852 the Society paid $4,205 to cut and dress the marble manually. To have dressed the same amount of marble by machinery, Dougherty said, would have cost only $3,310, a considerable savings. No evidence indicates that Dougherty ever convinced the building committee.[32]

Soon after Symington began work under his contract, he discovered that the railroad did not have enough cars to transport all of his marble. Delays caused rough stone to accumulate at the quarry. At one point Symington complained that he had to stop quarrying because he had no room to store the marble awaiting transportation. At the monument site the delay kept stonecutters and masons idle.[33]

The building committee ran up against expenses that had not been calculated during contract negotiations. The blocks of marble for the cornices of the two large doorways led to unexpected expenses. When quarrymen accidentally split ashler marble, as they frequently did, they made simple adjustments and ultimately used nearly every split block. On the other hand, when quarrymen removed unusually shaped blocks for cornices and architraves, they took extreme pains to prevent a split because that would make the stone unusable. Although not necessarily greater in weight than the ashler stone, these blocks cost more. Also, a quarryman could quarry and handle 500 tons of ashler stone at less cost than a cornice or architrave block. Although unnegotiated and unmentioned in the contract, this inequity caused Symington to complain. The building committee decided to allow him $2 per foot for eight blocks of marble that he furnished for the doorways.[34]

There is little evidence of Mills' employment practices at the monument. Because of his duties as Architect of Public Buildings and his involvement in the construction of the Treasury Building, Patent Office, and Post Office at the time, he very likely left details of hiring employees to Dougherty, the superintendent of construction, with the concurrence of the building committee. Mills did insure that construction conformed to his design and specifications. Dougherty, who received his appointment in June 1848, handled much of the day-to-day supervision at the site, checking materials and overseeing their installation. The building committee appointed David Hepburn, who enjoyed a reputation as a skilled builder, as foreman under Dougherty. Hepburn was largely responsible for directing the construction of the foundation. During the first year of construction, when the Society concentrated on the foundation, a relatively small crew worked on the monument—14 stonemasons, 2 stonecutters, 4 carpenters, and 1 rigger. By December 1849, 57 men worked regularly at the site.[35]

Wages for the workers in those years reveal the basic differences between supervisory, skilled, and unskilled staff. Hepburn, the foreman, received $2.50 a day. A mastermason got $2.00 a day, blacksmiths $1.75, carpenters $1.00 to $2.00, and ordinary laborers $1.00. By 1851 stonecutters received $2.25 a day, but laborers still got only $1.00, an indication of how poorly the unskilled worker fared.[36]

Excavations for the foundation began in the spring of 1848. In May the board of managers advertised for gneiss stone from the quarries of the Potomac Valley. The gneiss was to be large, durable, not less than 4 feet square, and 9 to 12 inches thick. The stones were to cover 1,600 to 3,600 feet.[37] Mills described the foundation for the 500-foot shaft in an 1848 article:

> The foundation [is] built with massive stones of the firmest texture, the blue rock of the Potomac Valley, many of the blocks of which weigh from six to eight tons, and which come out of the quarry in square masses, as if cut with the tool, and of varied shapes, so that when laid in the foundation they allow and are made to dovetail into each other, forming thereby a stronger mass of masonry than if the same were squared up as in regular masonry. The mortar used in bedding and binding the stones is composed of hydraulic cement and strong stone lime, with their proper proportion of coarse sharp sand, which will become as hard as the stone it binds in a very few weeks. Every crevice of the stone is filled up with this mortar, and

grouted. The square or footing of this foundation for the obelisk is eighty feet each way, and rising by offsets or steps twenty five feet high, the whole built of solid masonry, upon which the obelisk shaft will be placed.[38]

Mills and the building committee had a serious responsibility for the safety of the foundation and the obelisk. After the workmen completed the foundation, the committee and Mills invited a group of 12 to 15 architects, engineers, and other experts to make a final inspection of the foundation before construction of the superstructure got underway. According to Thomas Carbery, chairman of the building committee, the entire group expressed the highest confidence in the foundation, noting that "it could not be better."[39]

Mills, who was present at the inspection, later wrote:

> Every precaution was taken to test the understrata where the foundations were laid. A well was dug some little distance, which indicated favorably; the strata was found very compact, requiring a pick to break it up, and at the depth of twenty feet a solid bed of gravel was reached, and six feet lower an abundant supply of the finest water was obtained.
>
> Though the indication were [sic] satisfactory, the architect of the work directed a shaft to be sunk in the centre of the foundation, twenty feet below the bottom of the same, and the same results took place as in the case of the well.
>
> This shaft was also walled up, and has served a good purpose in keeping the foundations dry, and will serve a valuable one hereafter in furnishing a full supply of excellent water as the work goes up; as, by means of a force pump, it could be sent up to the top of the monument, thus supplying a refreshing beverage to the workmen, as well as meeting the demands of the work for water.[40]

With the foundation in place, on 4 July 1848 workmen laid the cornerstone of the shaft amid considerable fanfare. Thomas Symington, the marble contractor, donated the block. Symington took meticulous care in removing the cornerstone from the quarry, transporting it safely and on time to the site, and dressing it. The stone was 6.5 square feet by about 2.5 feet thick and weighed 24,500 pounds. For this occasion, everyone donated his services. The Susquehanna and Baltimore Railroad shipped the stone to Washington free. On its arrival, a large body of workmen from the Washington Navy Yard, assisted by other citizens who volunteered their services, transported the stone to the site. Mathew G. Emery, a stonemason and contractor who later became mayor of Washington, cut and dressed the stone free of charge. He cut a sizeable hole in the stone for a zinc case filled with memorabilia associated with the event.[41]

Many dignitaries attended the ceremony. In addition to members of the Society and Mills, the guests included President James Polk; Speaker of the House of Representatives Robert C. Winthrop, who gave the oration;

James K. Polk. *Library of Congress.*

several ranking federal, state, and diplomatic officials; Alexander Hamilton's widow; and Dolley Madison, wife of the fourth President of the United States. The press noted that the ceremonies "surpassed in magnificence and moral grandeur anything of the kind ever witnessed in this metropolis, since the formation of the Republic." The workmen laid the cornerstone at the northeast angle of the foundation.[42]

Aside from the early problems of transporting the rough marble from the quarries, construction progressed normally. Robert Mills could boast as early as September 1848, not long after the workmen laid the cornerstone, that "the foundations are now brought up nearly to the surface of the ground; the second step being nearly completed, which covers up the corner stone." He added that "about two thousand perches of stone are laid, and it is expected the foundations will be all ready for the stone work before the winter sets in."[43]

Work on the superstructure must have started nearly on schedule, for by the end of 1852 the shaft reached 126 feet.[44] In September 1854 Superintendent Dougherty outlined the state of construction in some detail to the chairman of the building committee, advising him to take certain measures to insure progress. Dougherty explained that:

> there is now on the ground 835 feet face measurement or about 1500 cubic feet of marble which will make 2 additional courses and leave a balance of 51 feet face measurement which by the 1st of October will be increased to about 150 feet, leaving 240 feet required to make an additional course....

The funds on hand affected construction, and Dougherty's job was to keep the building committee informed not only of progress but also of any additional work that could be accomplished economically. Thus, he felt constrained to give the chairman the following advice:

> It would be very desirable could the marble which is now laying on the ground cut be set in the building as it will be liable to in-

> jury should it be suffered to remain on the ground.... have spoken to the men and told them the probability of the work being stopped on the 1st of October. They agree should the Board permit them to continue to take any portion of their wages (no matter how small) which it may be convenient to pay them and to wait for the balance until funds were collected, so that by an outlay of say $1000, between the 1st of November and the 1st of December, all the stone now cut could be set in the building, leaving none but the rough marble on the ground which could not be injured....[45]

The spectre of declining contributions always haunted the Society. Although it had agreed to the Mills plan for an obelisk as high as 600 feet, limited funds forced the Society to fix the height at 500 feet. If additional money became available, the Society would build the monument to its original proposed height. Carbery, chairman of the building committee, explained that the cost to erect only 500 feet was $375,000 but the price for 600 feet was $475,000. These figures did not include construction of the iron stairway and platforms or any work on the grounds surrounding the obelisk.[46]

Memorial Stones

In 1849 some citizens from Alabama proposed to quarry and dress a block of marble from that state and present it to the Society as a gift for the inside of the monument. This proposal induced the Society to adopt a policy that, at first, appeared beneficial but later proved unfortunate. The Society thought it proper to represent all the states and territories at the monument by having them contribute memorial stones that would be fitted into the interior walls. The Society hoped that the memorial stones might compensate for the lack of funds. In any event, the states willingly donated, and blocks of stone—marble, granite, sandstone, and other durable stones—arrived at the site from all parts of the country.

Later the Society permitted Indian tribes, societies, professional organizations, labor unions, businesses, individuals, and even foreign countries to donate memorial stones. The Society limited the size of the stones to 4 feet long, 2 feet high, and 12 to 18 inches thick, and suggested inscriptions, such as the name of the state or donor and, if desired, the coat of arms. However, the instructions were often vague, and donors submitted all sizes and types of lettering and inscriptions. Stones from foreign countries, including China, France, Greece, and England, arrived with inscriptions in their respective languages. In short, uniformity was frequently sacrificed.[47]

Some groups went to extensive pains to raise the money necessary to provide a stone. The American Medical Association, meeting in Richmond, Virginia, in 1852 appointed a committee to issue a circular to all its

The Washington Monument in 1853, as shown in *Gleason's Pictorial Drawing-Room Companion*. Library of Congress (photograph USZ62-32301).

members soliciting $1 donations. Some entrepreneurs were evidently more interested in advertising their product than in paying tribute to their national hero. The Society inserted these stones in the walls along with the rest.[48]

The Society attached considerable importance to the formalities surrounding the acceptance of memorial stones. Delegations from the various states and foreign governments, and frequently even the President of the United States, were present to dedicate a donated stone.[49]

By 1855 the Society had installed 92 stones in the rising walls of the shaft's interior. Each of the states and two territories had made their contributions. More memorial stones arrived than could be emplaced, so the Society temporarily stored them in the lapidarium.[50]

Contributions Fade and Work Is Halted

By the end of 1854, six years after construction began, the Society had exhausted its funds. Internal dissension within the Society, the serious economic conditions of the times, and the political turmoil that would culminate in the Civil War prevented the Society from raising more money.

By 1854 the Society had spent $230,000. The board of managers presented a memorial to Congress that described the state of construction and explained that all recent efforts to obtain funds had failed. The Society was asking Congress for help, but it could not have chosen a more inappropriate time. Congress could not do anything to ameliorate the situation, nor was it so inclined, and so the matter rested.[51]

By the time work stopped in 1854, the shaft had risen to 152 feet. It measured 55 feet and 1.5 inches on each of its four sides. The shaft tapered upward so that each side at the top measured nearly 49 feet. The center of the obelisk, which formed the well, measured 25 feet and 1 inch on each side. The masonry consisted of a large crystal white marble facing and a blue gneiss stone rubble backing. The marble facing varied from 14 to 18 inches thick in courses of 2 feet rise. The stretchers outran the headers, which were about 6 feet long, with no attempt to obtain a regular bond. The thickness of the walls at the top was almost 12 feet and at the base was about 15 feet. The weight of the partially completed shaft was estimated at about 31,152 tons.[52]

As conceived in his plan, Mills built two entrances to the monument, one facing east and the other west. Designed with an Egyptian motif, they were 15 feet high and 6 feet wide. A heavy pediment and an entablature displaying a carved winged ball and asp surmounted each doorway. These designs were consistent with the massive pantheon included in the original Mills design for the base of the obelisk.[53]

The foundation of the shaft was 80 feet square on each side of the bed. This bed was 7.67 feet below the general level of the ground, 23.34 feet thick, and 58.5 feet long on each side at the top. It extended upward in eight steps, resembling a truncated cone. The foundation consisted of bluestone gneiss. Spawls and mortar composed largely of lime and sand filled the interstices between the stones.[54] With the exception of a very small section added to the walls, the monument remained in this unfinished state for more than two decades, much to the embarassment of many Americans.

Chapter III

THE INTERREGNUM

The economic conditions and the political turmoil of the 1850s kept the Society from raising enough funds for the monument. The controversy that raged between the North and South as they slowly approached war made any consistent or prolonged attempt to raise money extremely difficult. The internal affairs of the Washington National Monument Society had an even more direct effect upon fund raising. Congress accused the Society of mismanaging its funds and using them to buy petty services and trivia. Such charges impugned the integrity of the Society, which, in answering Congress, was frequently placed on the defensive.[1]

The Pope's Stone

But for two events, Congress would have supplied funds despite its general mistrust of the Society. In 1854, the Roman Pontiff, head of the Roman Catholic Church and ruler of the small Italian Papal States, indicated his willingness to contribute a memorial stone to the monument. As early as 1852, the Pope had revealed that a stone from the Temple of Concord in Rome would be sent. Certain anti-Catholic groups in America that despised anything that carried the Pontiff's blessing strongly protested. An 1852 pamphlet argued that the Society should not accept the stone because the Pope was a foreign tyrant. This same publication expressed the fear that as more Catholics migrated to America, the Pope would gain enough power to some day reign here. Fanatical messages of this nature and other expressions of bigotry flooded the Society, urging that the stone not be accepted.[2]

Much of this opposition to the Pope's Stone stemmed from the Know-Nothing Party, formed to prevent immigrants, especially Catholics, from entering the country. The party had its largest following in Baltimore and Washington. In 1854 Washington elected John T. Towers, a Know-Nothing, as mayor.[3] Having made some political headway, this party flexed its muscles at the Washington National Monument Society with impunity.

Despite strong opposition, the Pope's Stone arrived at the monument site in 1854. It was temporarily stored in the lapidarium where two armed guards were stationed at all times. During the early hours of 6 March 1854, several members of the Know-Nothing Party overpowered the guards and removed the stone. They carried it to the river where they broke off some pieces for souvenir hunters before tossing the rest into the water.

This vandalism created a considerable national stir. The Society offered a reward of $100 for any information leading to the arrest of the vandals. It also fired the watchman after concluding that he was part of the conspiracy.[4] There was no doubt that serious damage had been done to the Society's cause. Anger was widespread among Catholics, who rightfully felt that the vandalism had been directed at them, and among Protestants, who looked suspiciously upon the motives of the Know-Nothings. As a result, contributions to the Society, already meager, ceased altogether.

Control of the Society

The Society's situation could not have been worse in 1854. Nevertheless, its cause might have succeeded had not yet another unfortunate event occurred the next year. In 1854 the Society had appealed to Congress for assistance in raising the money needed to complete the monument. Some in Congress were still receptive, although most lacked faith in the Society. The House of Representatives referred the request to a select committee of 13. On 22 February 1855, chairman Henry May of the committee made an impassioned plea in behalf of the Society, recommending that Congress donate $200,000 to the beleaguered organization. He made it clear that this sum was to be only a contribution towards the monument; Congress did not intend to assume the full expense of building it.[5]

Just as it appeared that Congress would appropriate the $200,000, the Know-Nothings seized control of the Washington National Monument Society. The party called a meeting on the evening of 22 February 1855, which was contrary to the by-laws of the organization, and packed it with Society members who were also members of the party. Arguing that the Society had hired too many foreign born and Catholics, they elected new officers and a new board of managers sympathetic to their political and social views. Superintendent Dougherty refused to acknowledge the authority of the new board of managers and boarded up all the temporary buildings at the monument site to prevent their takeover. The new board ultimately replaced him with Samuel Briggs.[6]

For three years the two societies existed side by side. During that time the old board of managers made every effort to resolve the matter but to no avail. The new board adamantly insisted on its legitimacy. It accused the old board of withholding information and records needed to run the organization; not delivering the treasurer's books and papers; not informing the new board of contracts; permitting tools and machinery to deteriorate; and allowing the marble supply to become exhausted.[7]

Fortunately, as the power and successes of the American Party waned, so did its influence over the Society. The Know-Nothings finally relinquished their control over the Society in 1858 after an unsuccessful attempt to raise money. In the three years they controled the monument, they added only 26 feet of masonry, marble that the master mason had originally rejected as imperfect.[8]

This second embarassing episode taught the Society that an organization designed to collect funds on a national scale could not manage its affairs by a voluntary association of members living so far apart. In 1859, one year after the old board resumed control, Congress wisely incorporated the Society. With this new legality to strengthen and support it, the Society was prepared to move ahead with its fund raising. The ill-fated attempt to gain congressional support for funds, begun in 1855, had to wait another four years. By then it was too late—the war was fast approaching.

Meanwhile, the Society tried to revive public interest and obtain aid for completion. It devised a plan to secure contributions from voters at all municipal and general elections and sought appropriations from state legislatures. Through circular letters, it asked for aid from all political, corporate, or voluntary bodies; the United States Army and Navy; societies; churches; and individuals. Despite these well-meaning efforts, little money trickled into the Society's coffers. At a general election in Washington on 6 June 1859, the Society received contributions amounting to only $150.76.[9] Although appeals for funds were made by the Society from time to time with some minor successes, responses soon stopped completely. The nation torn by a civil war turned its attention towards more pressing matters.

The lack of funds and the conflicts that existed among the old board of managers reopened the question of the foundation's safety and the appropriateness of the design. Despite strong opposition, the Society felt an obligation to the people who had supported the monument project and fought courageously to retain the site and what had been completed. Although the Society had modified the original Mills design, much of this alteration was aimed at forestalling any further temporizing. Lack of funds justified this change. "Let the present generation," said Congressman May in 1855, "at least complete the shaft, and we may then permit those who come after us to finish the whole work."[10] Thus, by 1859, the Mills design had not been abandoned, but only altered to accomodate the current state of finances.

The foundation was a different matter entirely. The foundation had already been built, and the Society had to counter criticisms concerning its safety by calling on engineers and scientists to convince the public of its safety. In 1859, having been given renewed vitality by its congressional charter, the Society asked Secretary of War John Floyd to assign an Army Engineer to examine the foundation. Lieutenant Joseph C. Ives of the Corps of Engineers was selected for this work.

Lieutenant Ives was born in New York City, and graduated from the United States Military Academy in 1852. Early in his career he had been appointed commander of an expedition to explore the Colorado River. The Army later appointed him astronomer and surveyor to a commission that surveyed the boundary between California and the adjacent territories. After his brief but important assignment to the Washington National Monument, he joined the Confederacy and was appointed chief engineer of the coastlines of South Carolina, Georgia, and East Florida. Later he became aide-de-camp to President Jefferson Davis of the Confederacy.[11]

Ives' principal duty at the monument was to study the stability and safety of the foundation. In his report to the Society, he stated that he could not detect any signs of settling or insecurity. The only defects he found were a few chipped blocks of marble in the lowest courses of the shaft, the result of joints being laid too close together. He believed, however, that an adequate base could hide these defective joints.[12] Lieutenant Ives' findings only temporarily alleviated some of the doubts about the foundation's stability. The issue was to be raised again and again.

Although associated with the Society only briefly, Ives also became involved in fund raising. Whether the Society originally intended this or whether Ives later assumed this responsibility, is not clear. In any event, soon after he tested the foundation and reported his results, he became embroiled in fund-raising activities. One writer has said that the Secretary of War permitted him to hold the position of treasurer for the Society while also carrying out his engineering duties. Such a position seems odd for a military person on active duty. Moreover, the Society's historian does not refer to such an appointment. He does say that Ives submitted a plan to raise funds by erecting contribution boxes in post offices throughout the country and designating postmasters as agents for the Society to care for and supervise the funds. At the end of the four months the plan was in operation, the Society collected $2,240 from 841 post offices, far short of its goal. By the end of 1859, the Society's total receipts amounted to only $3,075.[13]

No one could accuse the Society of apathy toward fund raising, but it was difficult to overcome the general public indifference. Construction on the monument had stopped long ago, and the Civil War halted collections. Now the Society had to preserve what had been completed.

During the war the unfinished monument symbolized the break between the states. Union soldiers drilled on the monument grounds. In 1861 the Union Army notified the Society that it needed the grounds to graze cattle to feed the troops. The Army also stored hay in the temporary structures and constructed a slaughterhouse nearby. The Army fenced in the grounds to prevent the cattle from wandering off, but this did not keep Southern sympathizers from communicating with Virginia pickets and intimidating government clerks around the unfinished monument.[14] On 22 February

The monument grounds in 1862, as depicted in *Leslie's Illustrated Newspaper.*
Library of Congress (photograph USZ62-59908).

1862, in what was considered to be a heroic feat, a rigger from the Navy Yard ascended the walls of the monument by rope, hand-over-hand, and placed a Union flag at the summit.[15]

At the end of the war, the unfinished monument and its grounds, like the rest of Washington, had been seriously neglected and remained a sorry spectacle. Surrounded by the rubble of broken stones and the debris from the cattle pens and slaughter house, the stump of the monument became an eyesore and a symbol of civic decay. Mark Twain caustically referred to it as a "factory chimney with the top broken off."[16]

In the meantime, the Society tried to begin where it had left off before the war. With renewed vigor, it called attention to the unfinished monument. A large number of people attended its first postwar meeting, on 22 February 1866. President Andrew Johnson, presiding at the meeting, gave a stirring speech. "Let us restore," he said, "the Union, and let us proceed with the Monument as its symbol until it shall contain the pledge of all the States of the Union."[17] Although construction of the monument was one of the few issues that North and South could agree upon, his words, like those of the Society, were ignored.

During the postwar years the Society tried fruitlessly to obtain an appropriation from Congress. As before the war, it sought the aid of state and territorial legislatures as well as private groups and individuals, but the attempts failed abysmally. In criticizing the apparent lack of patriotism in Americans, one writer said:

> There never has been a time when this amount can be raised so easily. The country is full of money, and millions are yearly expended in extravagence [sic] and folly. A little more genuine patriotism would relieve the nation from the ridiculous position in which this unfinished structure places it.[18]

Unfortunately, the problem was deeper than that. The nation was still reeling from the effects of the war; it would take years before the wounds would heal.

Chapter IV

REVIVAL OF INTEREST

Marshall's Investigations

Isolated voices occasionally decried the lack of interest in the monument and encouraged the nation to revive its efforts to build a memorial to Washington. *The New York Herald* called the unfinished monument "a disgrace to our people," and urged that it be completed immediately. The newspaper suggested a plan to reward individuals or corporations that contributed $1,000 to $5,000 by inscribing their names on a block of stone in the monument. Also, the Society's archives should maintain a list of those contributing $100 to $500. Some business organizations generously offered their services and material. One marble company offered to contribute all

The monument in 1878, standing as it had for 25 years. *Library of Congress (photograph BH823-2).*

the marble necessary to complete the monument if the Society assumed the quarrying and transportation expenses.[1] Many of these proposals were unrealistic, and some even bordered on the ridiculous, but they did indicate a strong sentiment in the country to complete the monument.

In spite of the many postwar social and economic problems, interest in the monument gained momentum because of the country's forthcoming centennial. Speeches about the celebration flooded congressional halls. Newspapers all over the country saw the centennial as an opportunity to promote and hold interest in the monument. The Washington National Monument Society felt that it should seek congressional aid immediately. The Society opposed returning to the old system of relying on contributions, at least until construction continued. In a letter to the chairman of the House Committee for the District of Columbia, the secretary of the Society, John Carroll Brent, appealed to Congress for an appropriation so that work could resume. The House of Representatives received the request and on 27 January 1873 appointed a select committee to confer with the Society on how best to complete the monument in time for the centennial celebration.[2]

In less than a month the committee presented its report, concluding that the time was propitious for congressional action. After reviewing the monument's long history and agreeing on the suitability of the design and site, the committee reaffirmed the Society's belief that the elaborate and costly pantheon surrounding the shaft was not essential to the completion of the obelisk itself and could be added later. The committee concluded that the obelisk, "This rich and massive shaft, though simple and plain, would be a noble monument, worthy of the sublime character which it is designed to testify."[3]

Before the select committee submitted its report it wisely asked technical experts about the foundation's stability. Norton P. Chipman, chairman of the committee, asked Major General Andrew A. Humphreys, the Army's Chief of Engineers, whether there was any reason to question

Andrew A. Humphreys.
Library of Congress.

the stability of the monument's foundation. Chipman wondered if the foundation had shifted or settled since Lieutenant Ives had tested it in 1859 and asked Humphreys to have a competent engineer examine the foundation. Chipman also requested estimates of the costs to complete the monument and build a plain but suitable base instead of a pantheon.[4]

Humphreys detailed First Lieutenant William Louis Marshall to this project. A young and bright engineer, Marshall presented his results within a few days. A graduate of the United States Military Academy in 1868, Marshall later distinguished himself in other areas of engineering and in western explorations. He became the Chief of Engineers in 1908. Marshall believed it was "practicable at present to present only the results of a necessarily hasty and superficial inspection of the monument and its foundation course."[5] Although Marshall studied Ives' report, the Society's records did not contain the original experiments and investigations conducted by Mills and his colleagues. This lack of information created a serious problem for engineers and other experts assigned to examine the monument in the 1870s.

Why the select committee gave Marshall so little time to investigate and report on a problem that they obviously considered a serious one remains a mystery. In any event, Marshall generally agreed with Ives' 1859 report. His examination failed to reveal any significant changes in the condition of the obelisk or its foundation. He objected to the blue gneiss stone in the foundation, which was not sufficiently uniform in texture and strength. He believed that dressed stone offered the greatest resistance to compression and would distribute the weight more uniformly over the bed of the foundation. Finally, he concluded that "all questions as to the stability of the shaft itself have been answered by Lieutenant Ives, in whose conclusion I concur." Marshall confessed that because of insufficient time, he could not estimate the cost of completion of the obelisk. He recommended building a simple, primarily earth terrace with a paved upper surface, "presenting the appearance of a massive obelisk shooting vertically from the solid earth."[6]

The select committee approved Marshall's report. Like Ives, Marshall presented "sufficient [evidence] that there is no ground for fear which has been expressed as to the security of the foundations." The committee recommended a congressional appropriation of $200,000 to help the Society begin its work, but estimated that it would cost about $700,000 to complete the shaft and provide a simple terrace. The committee thought that the Society could complete the obelisk in time for the centennial. Finally, the committee recommended that further Congressional appropriations be conditional on a competent engineer's thorough examination of the existing structure to determine if it could be safely built to a height of 600 feet.[7]

Although the committee accepted Marshall's study, others in Congress doubted the foundation's safety. The committee realized that it had given the Corps of Engineers and Marshall too little time to prepare a thorough and comprehensive study. Because it was anxious to receive an appropriation as soon as possible, it tentatively approved Marshall's report pending further examination.

Congress adjourned before it could act on the proposed bill, but at the next session in January 1874, it reappointed the select comittee to consider the monument question.[8] Not entirely satisfied with the Marshall report, the committee sought additional information from the Corps. It couched the new request in the same general terms as the first one, but it also asked for the cost and practicability of completing the shaft with brick in the interior. Furthermore, the committee wanted a precise estimate of the cost to complete a terrace at the base of the obelisk of approximately 4,000 square feet, rising about 17 feet, and containing steps and suitably paved approaches. Once again, it anxiously inquired whether the monument could be completed in time for the centennial.[9]

Marshall received this second task after returning from his western explorations. He now had more time to conduct field investigations, consult with experts, and finish the report. Three months later, on 20 April 1874, Marshall submitted his findings—a much more critical study than his earlier one. Basically, he repeated his earlier conclusion that the foundation was secure. He recommended a maximum height of only 400 feet because the foundation was too small to support a 600-foot structure. A monument of that size would cause "an excessive pressure upon a soil not wholly incompressible." Marshall was quite sure that "as far as can be discovered in a careful examination of the structure, there are no sufficient grounds for doubting the security of the foundation under the present load."

To minimize the weight of the shaft on the foundation, he proposed reducing the thickness of the walls from 11.46 to 7.3 feet and using a hard brick filling bonded at 30-foot intervals. He recommended that the Society construct the roof of the obelisk with cast-iron plates supported by wrought-iron beams and rods rather than with cloistered arches of stone. Finally, he proposed that the upper 200 to 250 feet of the shaft be constructed of brick, especially where the walls became thinner.[10]

Although Marshall's report failed to provide a cost estimate or a date for completion, it recommended some things that the select committee had not requested. Some of Marshall's suggestions, such as constructing the top 200 feet with brick and employing cast iron for the roof, were alien to the Mills design, and may have been objected to by Congress, the Society, and architectural circles. Generally the study met with approval because it supported the idea of retaining what was already built. The select committee agreed that a shorter obelisk "would be more graceful, and would be equally satisfactory to the American people." It suggested a height of 437 feet, to which Marshall agreed. The committee also felt that a terrace would not only be "more harmonious" with the style of the monument than the

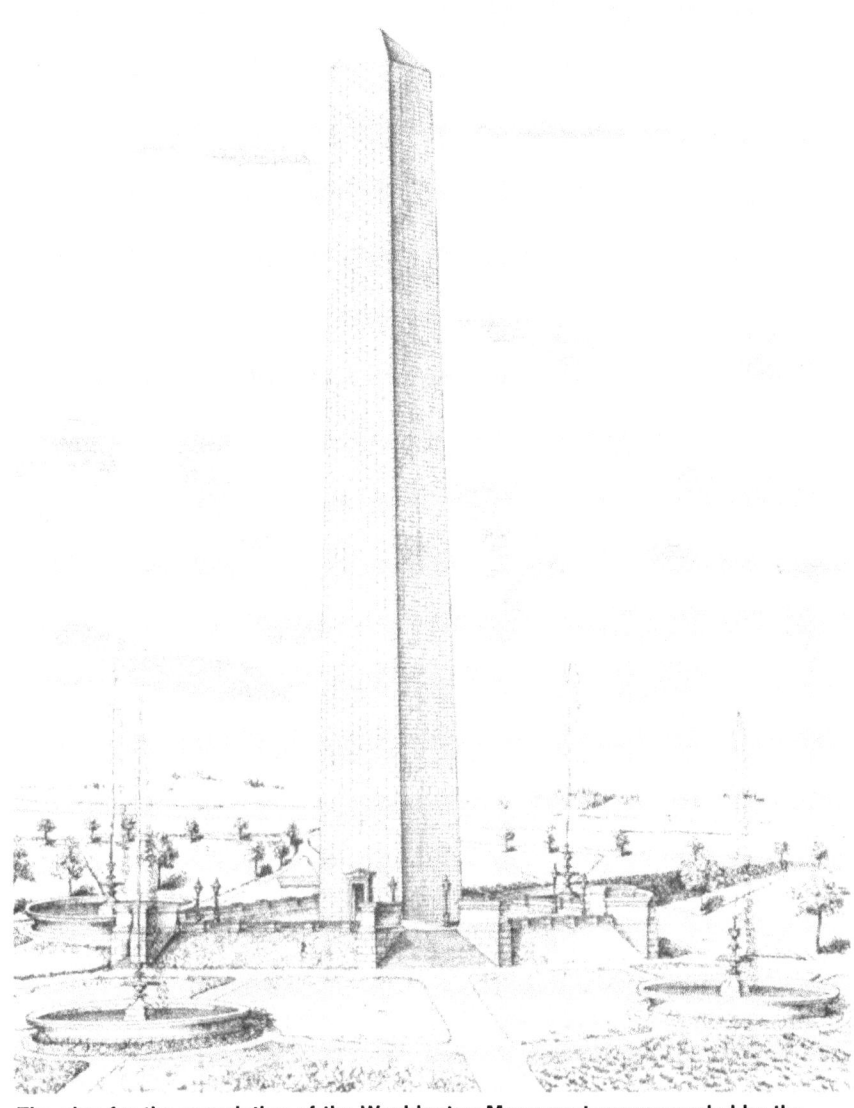
The plan for the completion of the Washington Monument recommended by the Select Committee of the House of Representatives. *Library of Congress (photograph USZ62-3968).*

original pantheon, which had elicited such strong criticism, but also more economical. On 1 May 1874, the committee rendered its report to Congress, along with Marshall's study, recommending passage of a joint resolution to provide a sufficient appropriation to complete the monument by 4 July 1876.[11]

As it had done so many times before, Congress failed to act. Time was running out with the centennial only two years away. Convinced that Congress would never come to its aid in time, the Society again appealed for funds.[12] Not expecting to be any more successful than in the past, the Society hoped it might shame Congress into passing an appropriation.

Congressional and public opposition to the monument centered around the foundation and the design. Many, especially in Congress, remained unconvinced that the foundation was safe. The plain obelisk contrasted sharply with Victorian principles of art and design. One newspaper referred to the monument as "a wretched design, a wretched location, and an insecure foundation."[13]

To allay congressional fears about the foundation's safety, Chipman requested Marshall to clarify further his statements on the foundation. Chipman did not believe that Marshall had been clear enough. Although the Engineer had recommended a lower height, he had not satisfied Congress that this shorter structure would still be safe on the existing foundation. Chipman was certain that if this point was clarified, Congress would pass an appropriation at its next session. Marshall quickly replied. Without examining the foundation further, he stated unequivocally that the monument could be built safely to 400 feet. He concluded by saying that "this is simply an individual opinion, and it is well to remark that the pressure will still be about as great as the maximum usually considered proper for such foundations."[14]

Perhaps it was unfair to ask one person to render an opinion of this magnitude, even one with Marshall's ability. Without seeking the committee's advice, the Corps of Engineers transmitted Marshall's report to the Board of Engineers for Fortifications, headquartered in New York City, for an evaluation. The board consisted of Brevet Major Generals John G. Barnard, Zealous B. Tower, and Horatio G. Wright.[15] Without making any field examinations, the board noted that according to Marshall's report the earth upon which the masonry foundation rested was already subject to a pressure of 4.8 tons per square foot of surface and had already settled some. The board reasoned that raising the shaft to 400 or more feet would add 1.8 tons more to each square foot of the earth's surface, thereby increasing the pressure. It concluded that "it is reasonable to infer that some subsidence will ensue from so large an increase." The board felt that five tons was an excessive pressure for soils composed of clay and sand to bear. "We could not...with the information before us, recommend that any *additional* pressure should be thrown on the site of the Washington Monument."[16]

The Board's conclusions disturbed the select committee, which had already accepted Marshall's findings. They also provided the skeptics in Congress and elsewhere with additional ammunition. General Humphreys concurred with the board and recommended that the Society make extensive borings around the foundation to determine the thickness and extent of any subsidence in the substratum. He then opened a Pandora's Box by suggesting consideration of another design that would place less pressure on the existing foundation. Humphreys proposed that "means be taken to obtain from architects...designs for finishing off the present shaft by some suitable terminal, and possibly by addition at the angles of the column."[17] This started an "esthetic argument seldom equaled in gentlemenly virulence, and a series of substitute designs unsurpassed for ambitious vacuity."[18]

Congress Passes an Appropriation and Appoints a Joint Commission

The Board's conclusions further slowed progress in a Congress that already had been procrastinating. The approaching centennial and the news media, which produced a barrage of stinging attacks, most of them directed at Congress, eventually ended the impasse. Although the action came too late to finish the structure in time for the centennial, on 2 August 1876, Congress finally passed a $200,000 appropriation to resume construction. The act stipulated that the Society would have to convey all rights, property, and easements to the United States, but would continue to solicit funds and act as an adviser in building and maintaining the monument. The act authorized the appointment of a Joint Commission to oversee construction. This commission, later referred to as the Joint Commission on the Construction of the Washington National Monument, was to consist of five members, including the President of the United States, the Supervising Architect of the Treasury Department, the Architect of the Capitol, the Chief of Engineers of the Corps of Engineers, and the First Vice-President of the Washington National Monument Society. The act also provided that before any work began on the monument, experts would examine the foundation to determine whether it was strong enough to sustain the completed structure. If these experts found the foundation inadequate, Congress was to be notified so that it could take appropriate measures.[19]

Congressional opposition to the appropriation stemmed from objections to the foundation, site, or design. The provision to examine the foundation before any work began partially mitigated objections about the foundation's weaknesses. However, the bill did little to satisfy critics of the design and site. During the debates, one senator called the design a "blot upon architecture."[20] Many suggested that they completely demolish the unfinished monument and build a new one designed in a more Victorian style.

On 30 March 1876, the Society declared that "all idea of surrendering the character of the Monument or allowing the structure, as far as completed, to be taken down, should be positively and emphatically disavowed."[21] The Society thereby fulfilled an obligation to those who had made their contributions to the monument through the years believing that the structure would be built according to the Mills design, albeit somewhat modified. However courageous the Society's stand on this issue, it did not stop the criticism.

On 12 September 1876, the Joint Commission on the Construction of the Washington National Monument met to organize in the offices of the Society. William W. Corcoran, First Vice-President of the Society, Edward Clark, Architect of the Capitol, and James G. Hill, Supervising Architect of the Treasury Department, attended the meeting. General Humphreys and the President could not attend. The commission appointed Corcoran president and Hill secretary. After selecting its officers, the commission immediately agreed to request the Secretary of War to appoint a board of engineers to examine the foundation as provided for in the act.[22]

William W. Corcoran. *Library of Congress.*

At its second meeting on 22 November the commission appointed General Humphreys disbursing agent. In the meantime, the Society, abiding by the provisions of the act, transferred the land, the unfinished obelisk, and all temporary structures, machinery, and materials to the United States.[23]

A Board of Engineers Rejects the Ives and Marshall Reports

The board of engineers appointed by the Corps of Engineers to examine the stability of the foundation consisted of Lieutenant Colonel John D. Kurtz, Lieutenant Colonel Quincy A. Gilmore, and Lieutenant Colonel James C. Duane.[24] The board immediately dispatched Engineer Second Lieutenant Dan C. Kingman to evaluate the monument's foundation. After reviewing Kingman's report, the board concluded that the stratum of sand and clay upon which the foundation rested was already loaded to the limit of prudence, if not to the limit of safety. The earth was not sufficiently resistant to compression to justify completing the monument to the modified height of 437 feet. Nor would another design correct this weakness in the foundation.

Second, the report stated that the added weight that would be placed at the top of the shaft would probably cause extensive spalling and splitting in the ashler marble at the base.

Third, the board noted that the foundation masonry was not spread sufficiently to safely carry the full weight of the shaft. If the spread of the foundation had been greater, the weight of the shaft would have been distributed over a wider area.

Finally, the board concluded that the soil had been compressed as much as 8 or 9 inches. There was evidence that the shaft was out of plumb, and the foundation courses showed an "increasing departure from horizontality." These imperfections would worsen as the structure rose, possibly not to a dangerous degree, but enough to make them discernible.

After outlining point by point what it objected to in the foundation, the board presented its opinion:

> But this structure is to be an exposition to the world of the estimate which is placed upon Washington by his countrymen. It is a great, bare obelisk, plain to severity, a conception perhaps most suitable to symbolize the great character it would commemorate, but for these very reasons, exacting in all its parts, and particularly in its foundations, all the perfection of elements and details that can be given to its material and workmanship. The stones which compose the foundation should be strong and perfect, truly shaped and accurately placed together. There should be no yielding of the parts, and no disturbance of the levels.
>
> Upon such a foundation, a monument could be reared fit to commemorate Washington, and worthy of the nation of whose foundations he was the chief master builder.[25]

The board did not confine itself to a study of the foundation. It found that the ashler marble had been too closely jointed on the exterior. As a result, a number of marble blocks had yielded under the pressure and broken in two transversely. Many other blocks were badly chipped and spalled along the horizontal joints.[26] Marshall and Ives had pointed out these same defects, but neither had emphasized the seriousness of this condition.

When the Joint Commission received the Engineers' report, it agreed not to take any action other than to have it printed and forwarded to the Society.[27] The Society did not receive the study with enthusiasm. It feared that if the report were taken seriously, all activity on the monument would cease and it would be years before any new interest could be generated. The Society appointed a review committee, which concluded that it "was not so exhaustive and satisfactory, as to relieve the subject from doubt." The committee believed that neither the Society nor the country would abandon the project because of a study that they characterized as containing "palpable" errors and that was at variance with earlier studies prepared by capable men.

The committee accused the Board of Engineers of not having given the study their personal attention and of having visited the site on only two or three occasions, each time remaining not more than an hour. It found unclear and contradictory statements in Lieutenant Kingman's field work. It admitted that a few of the marble blocks had cracked transversely, but the foundation remained essentially unchanged since 1853. The committee insisted that the foundation rested on "solid, compact clay" and not on a compressible bed of sand and clay as the Engineers had reported. The board's study contradicted all the facts and information in the Society's possession. The committee accused the board of concerning itself with matters that it was not asked to discuss: the board was to report only on the sufficiency of the foundation, not on the shaft or construction materials.

Finally, the committee charged the engineers with using the wrong stone as a bench mark for measuring the settlement of the structure. As a result, the settlement was registered at almost nine inches. The committee considered this a serious mistake. It concluded its review by saying that any inadequacy in the foundation could be remedied by underpinning and enlarging the area without injuring the existing structure.[28]

The committee's review, which received the Society's approval, belittled the ability of men highly esteemed in their professions. However justified it might have been on some points, the vitriolic tone weakened the report. Still, it is not difficult to understand the Society's reaction. For many years it had endured insults, embarassments, and failures, many of them unjustified. Its efforts to raise private and public funds, however ineffective, were well intentioned. Much of the failure to complete the monument rested with Congress. Moreover, the Ives and Marshall reports had suggested that any inadequacies in the foundation and the shaft could be remedied. After Congress finally passed the long-awaited appropriation, signaling the resumption of construction, the Board of Engineers dropped its bombshell. Society secretary John Blake explained that organization's frustrations. He said that no question had ever been raised about the foundation until years ago when some critics decided that the monument's design was not sufficiently ornate and offered other designs in its place. Blake complained that questions about the adequacy of the foundation stemmed from efforts to convince the public that the unfinished shaft should be torn down and another built in its place. He believed that the public was convinced that there was basically nothing seriously wrong with the foundation.[29]

On 31 May 1877, the Society forwarded the committee's reply to President Rutherford B. Hayes, suggesting that the committee and the Board of Engineers meet to reconcile their differences.[30]

The orders appointing the Board of Engineers did not require the board to recommend remedies if it found any defects in the foundation. To correct this omission, General Humphreys reconvened the board in New York City to consider widening the area of the foundation and carrying it down to the gravel bed beneath the compressible stratum of sand and clay. Six weeks later the board submitted its answer, suggesting two alternatives but recommending only one. The first proposed replacing the bed of clay and sand under the foundation with solid masonry. The board rejected this plan because of the delicate nature of the operation. The second plan consisted of circumscribing the existing foundation with a wall sufficiently thick and stable to resist any lateral movement of the soil that might occur with the added weight of the completed monument.[31]

Although the Corps of Engineers sought to make amends for its failure to recommend corrective measures for the foundation, the Society remained adamant and sought professional, scientific, and technical advice from other quarters. In a strongly worded letter to President Hayes, who had become involved in the monument's affairs as a member of the Joint Commission, the Society flatly stated that it neither concurred with the Engineers' findings nor approved of their remedy. Repeating what its three-member committee had already said, the Society accused the Engineers of using the wrong stone for a bench mark. Like Ives and Marshall, it believed that the foundation was safe and noted that during the past 20 years the shaft had stood at its present height without any evidence of "subsidence or of deflection from the vertical that is visible to the naked eye, or can be palpably detected by the use of the most delicate instruments."[32]

The Society blamed the adverse publicity against the foundation on a group of architects who found the Mills design to be "inappropriate" and "heathenish" and who preferred something more ornate. After receiving no public encouragement, the Society argued, this group first vented their objections on the site. Finding no support there, they objected to the foundation.[33]

The board admitted that it used the wrong stone as a bench mark. It said in its defense that the Society had directed them to that stone. In all other respects, the board held firm to its original findings, advising against additions to the shaft unless the Society added some underpinning of the kind suggested.[34]

By the end of October 1877, the Joint Commission had all of the board's reports as well as the Society's responses. In transmitting this data to Congress, the commission concluded that "it must be assumed that the foundation is insufficient to sustain the weight of the completed structure." Congress agreed. Another joint resolution, passed on 14 June 1878, authorized $36,000 to strengthen the foundation.[35]

Lieutenant Colonel Casey Takes Charge

Only a few days after Congress passed its appropriation for the foundation, the Joint Commission appointed two Army Engineers to assume charge of the project. Lieutenant Colonel Thomas Lincoln Casey, a career soldier with the Corps of Engineers, was to have complete control over construction. Captain George W. Davis, an engineer in the Infantry was to assist him in day-to-day operations. Casey's immediate superior, General Humphrey's, probably suggested Casey to the commission. Similarly, Casey probably recommended Davis as his assistant.[36]

Lieutenant Colonel Thomas Lincoln Casey.
Library of Congress.

Casey's background and career made him an excellent choice. He was born in Sackett's Harbor, New York, on 10 May 1831. His father, Brevet Major General Silas Casey, also had a distinguished military career. After graduating first in his class from West Point in 1852 and being commissioned in the Corps of Engineers, Casey's first assignment was to rebuild Fort Delaware. He afterwards returned to teach at West Point for five years. From November 1859 until 1861, the Army assigned him to Washington Territory supervising the construction of a road and selecting and surveying military reservations on Puget Sound. Soon after the outbreak of the Civil War, he was assigned to build the coastal defenses of Maine. There he made a name for himself by drawing most of the plans and developing his own skilled mechanics. Because of his accomplishments in this area, a private firm asked him to manage its plant. After seven months, he returned to the Army.

Due to his achievements with coastal defenses, in 1865 he was given the rank of brevet lieutenant colonel and was placed in charge of the Portland, Maine, Engineer Office. Beginning in November 1867 and for the next ten years, he headed the division of fortifications in the Office of the Chief of Engineers in Washington. A number of assignments in the capital gained him world-wide recognition. In March 1877, he became Superintending Engineer in Charge of Public Buildings and Grounds. He directed the construction of the State, War, and Navy Building, the Washington Aqueduct, the White House Conservatory, the Army Medical Museum, and other major works. Next to the monument, the State, War, and Navy Building was perhaps his greatest achievement.[37]

Davis' military career was different. Davis was born on 26 July 1839, in Thompson, Connecticut. In 1860 he became a tutor in Georgia, but the Civil War interrupted his teaching. The following year he escaped to the North, where he joined the 11th Connecticut Infantry and served in several campaigns. He remained in the Infantry after the war and became a brevet major. He was appointed captain in the Regular Army in 1867. While stationed in the Southwest he was placed in charge of building operations, after which he became Casey's assistant on the monument.

Bernard Richardson Green, a civilian with the Corps of Engineers,

Bernard Richardson Green.
Library of Congress.

assisted Casey and Davis. The three men had the highest mutual regard and worked well together. Green and Davis highly praised Casey's work. Davis, who spent much of his time at the monument administering contracts and handling the daily affairs of construction, frequently acted for Casey in the latter's absence, but always deferred a decision that he felt was beyond his authority. Many important and complicated features of the work performed during the construction of the monument were the result of suggestions made by both Davis and Green.

The print on his orders had barely dried when Casey wrote to Corcoran that he was reporting to the Joint Commission for further instructions. He suggested that two rooms in the building occupied by the Office of Public Buildings and Grounds at the corner of 17th and F streets Northwest (the Widener Building) become his office. As the Engineer in Charge of Public Buildings and Grounds, he was working in the building already. He wanted authority to supply the rooms as soon as possible with "such cheap office furniture as may be necessary." He also recommended hiring one clerk at $100 a month and one draftsman at $5 a day, the latter to be used only when needed. Finally, he proposed that all papers, plans, documents, and reports relating to the monument "should be placed in my hands" so that he could acquaint himself with all the data on the monument.[38]

At its next meeting the commission voted to allow Casey his office and furniture as well as permit him control over all papers and documents concerning the monument. It also directed him to submit to the commission for confirmation the names of people selected to appointments along with their salaries. Casey immediately hired A. L. Edwards as his clerk and Gustav Friebus as draftsman.[39]

On July 1, the commission instructed him to prepare a plan for strengthening the foundation so that he could raise the monument to at least 525 feet above the existing foundation. The commission also directed him to prepare a monthly progress and status report and a return of officers and hired men. These comprised a progress and status report. The commission also wanted monthly estimates of funds needed. Casey was to procure all materials by contract after advertising and receiving the approval of the commission.[40]

In October 1878, B. F. Navarre was appointed overseer at a salary of $150 a month. Two months later, the commission created a Building Committee, consisting of three members of the commission, to whom all matters relating to construction were referred. The Supervising Architect of the Treasury Department, the Architect of the Capitol, and the Chief of Engineers were appointed. Casey directed all his reports and queries to and received all his instructions from the Building Committee.[41]

The establishment of a Building Committee created a second layer of management in the administrative structure of the monument. If this added layer created any problems for Casey, it was not apparent. Because the

Building Committee was composed of architects and engineers, one of whom was Casey's superior, there was excellent rapport between him and the committee. It seldom interfered, preferring to give Casey a free hand.

Although Casey and the Building Committee were compatible, his relations with Corcoran, chairman of the Joint Commission, were less satisfactory, especially during the early period. The fact that Corcoran was both an officer of the Society and chairman of the commission complicated matters. Although Casey was subordinate to the commission, he had no direct connection with the Society other than when the latter advised the commission on some matter. Corcoran, an officer of both groups, sometimes confused his responsibilities and exercised unnecessary authority over Casey. The colonel resented these intrusions, which made him less tolerant of the Society.

The strained relationship at the beginning resulted from a misunderstanding over the Society's use of a room occupied by Casey and his clerk, who also happened to be an officer of the Society. Both the clerk and watchman of the monument were former employees of the Society. In July 1878, Corcoran managed to obtain employment for them with the understanding that the Society would continue to pay them. Casey understood, and rightly so, that these individuals would be under his supervision. When the secretary of the Society attempted to use his clerk for Society business during regular work hours, Casey objected, stating that if the Society needed his help, it would have to be given after the regular workday. The commission had neglected to inform Casey that it had arranged with the Society for the latter's use of the room for some of its business.[42] The fault seemed to rest with the commission for granting the Society office room without Casey's knowledge, especially when this space was in a building rented by the War Department for the Engineer in Charge of Public Buildings and Grounds and was space for which Casey was entirely responsible.

The Society found Casey's conduct in this matter offensive and asked the commission to look into the matter. The commission appointed a special committee, consisting of Humphreys and Clark, to examine the Society's allegations. Humphreys and Clark quickly dismissed the charges on the grounds that there had been a misunderstanding and that no disciplinary action should be taken against Casey. Moreover, the committee pointed out that Casey's services were "very valuable" to the commission.[43]

Although this incident was dropped, Casey's conduct disturbed both Corcoran and the Society on other occasions. Because Corcoran chaired the Joint Commission, his accusations could have had serious repercussions. In December 1878 Corcoran addressed a strongly worded letter to the commission outlining some of Casey's abuses in the hiring and firing of employees. He accused Casey of appointing and dismissing employees without the commission's authority and of disregarding a resolution passed earlier requiring him to make all appointments and dismissals above the rank of laborer and mechanic subject to the commission's approval. "The matter," said Corcoran, "is brought to the notice of the Commission that it may determine whether its orders are to be respected." The commission took no action against Casey other than to remind him of the resolution.[44]

Casey's Modifications to the Monument

One of the most serious problems that faced Casey, as it had others before him, was the absence of many of the principals who had been involved in the first stages of construction and the loss of early records and drawings. This prevented continuity and understanding of what had gone on before. Many of the records were lost in the 1850s during the struggle with the Know-Nothings. What were left to Casey were the later records that involved the Corps, writings in technical journals, and what one or two living principals remembered. In planning his next moves Casey had to rely mostly upon his sound judgment and deduction.

Casey confronted other serious problems, all stemming from the differences of opinion in Congress and in the Society concerning the adequacy of the foundation and the design. President Hayes took a personal interest in the monument and regularly attended the Joint Commission's meetings. He had much to do with the commission's decisions. Hayes recalled that Congress, the Society, and professional circles had two major objections.

Rutherford B. Hayes.
Library of Congress.

First, the foundation would not sustain an "average warehouse" and to strengthen it would be a mistake. Second, if the shaft were completed, it would be a disgrace to the nation—merely a tall and awkward smokestack at best. The shaft, these critics said, should be torn down and an arch or ornate structure filled with statues and allegorical figures built in its place.[45]

Shortly after Congress passed its appropriation and created the Joint Commission in 1876, the Society and the commission received several plans for strengthening the foundation and a new monument design. These plans found adherents particularly among those disturbed by the Mills design and those who, with greater justification, objected to the inadequate foundation. The recent scientific evidence supported critics of the foundation. Many of these were convinced that no amount of improvement could strengthen the foundation.

Fred E. Stuart of Washington prepared a plan to strengthen the foundation that gained much attention. It consisted of a series of brick arches laid in cement around the existing foundation. By the time Casey arrived on duty, Stuart had died, but his brother continued promoting the idea. Casey concluded that the plan contains "no feature which gives increased spread to the base of the foundation." The same amount of pressure as before would be placed on the bed of the foundation. Casey could not understand how the vertical arches and piers could materially increase the resistance of the soil under the monument to any lateral displacement.[46]

Meanwhile, Casey had received instructions to proceed with his own planning. In less than one month he solved the foundation problem. His plan considered the 525-foot obelisk, required by the commission. After carefully measuring and estimating the weight of the existing shaft, Casey concluded that the foundation could not hold the completed structure. Thus far, his findings coincided with those of the Board of Engineers. After reviewing the two proposals for securing the foundation, Casey decided to underpin and extend the surface of the base of the foundation. He began with a mass of Portland cement concrete, 126.5 feet square. The bottom

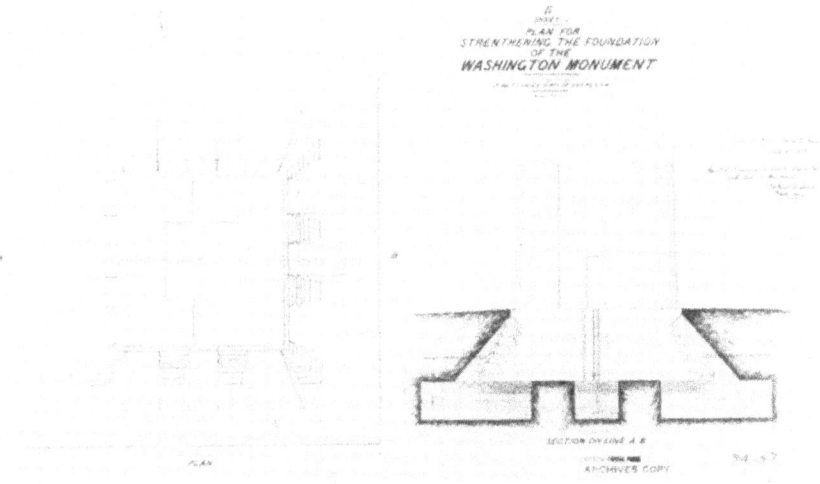

Casey's plans for strengthening the foundation with underpinning and buttressing.
National Archives (Record Group 79, file 74.1-1).

surface would be at the water level, or 12.33 feet below the bottom of the foundation. This mass would extend 18 feet under the outer edge of the foundation and 5 feet under the outer face of the shaft at its lowest joint.

The outer edges of this mass, 23.25 feet without the base, would be the foundation's edges. The mass would be 41.25 feet wide. The outer edges of this foundation would enclose 16,002 square feet. Three large buttresses on each side of the structure—12 in all—would lock the old foundation into the new and distribute the pressure more uniformly over the new mass. The buttresses would be carried from the upper surface of the new foundation up and under the outer portions of the shaft. A leg of concrete under the middle of the foundation would support it. If necessary two cross-walls of masonry under the center of the foundation would be built instead of the isolated mass.

The bed of the foundation, when the earth of the terrace reached the bottom of the shaft, would be subjected to the following pressure:

> Weight of foundations .... 21,160 tons.
> Weight of shaft........................ 43,671 tons.
> Weight of earth on top foundation .... 14,269 tons.
> Weight of earth within foundation .... 1,278 tons.
>
> Total .... 80,378 tons.

giving a mean pressure per square foot upon the bed of 5,022 tons.

Casey also noted in his report that wind might bring more pressure to bear on some parts of the monument's surface than others, although "the actual load on the foundation, or the bed of the foundation, is not increased." At the projected shaft and foundation, the maximum pressure per square foot on any part of the bed of the foundation would not exceed 5,398 tons, even with a wind pressure of about 55 pounds to the square foot. This pressure was only 0.371 of a ton greater than the pressure exerted by the old foundation:

> [considering] that the earth under the foundation will contain some 35 volumes less of clay, in excess of the voids in the sand, than the earth under the present foundation, and that the new bed of the foundation will be 35 feet 8 inches beneath the surface, while the present bed is but 7 feet 8 inches, it seems safe to recommend this foundation for the proposed shaft of 525 feet in height.

Casey was aware that any undertaking of this magnitude and difficulty required the utmost caution and skill. He noted that to undermine a structure that weighed nearly 32,000 tons and replace much of it with masonry "is evidently a delicate operation." The work could succeed "by introducing the masonry in thin, vertical layers," not more than four feet wide, by first tunneling under the structure with four-foot wide drifts that were high enough and long enough. Dowel stones set in the faces of the layers as the work progressed, and panel depressions in the alternate layers into which the intermediate layers would be molded would connect the layers. Casey planned to build the layers with strong Portland cement concrete except, possibly, for a short distance just under the old foundation, where rubble masonry would be forced in and wedged up under the stones of that structure.

Casey had not yet decided the order in which the tunnels would be run, "other than that they should be excavated in pairs on opposite sides of the monument, and in such a way that unequal strain shall not be brought upon the structure." After the foundation was completed, Casey recommended "a trial pressure, in which case the structure would be loaded with as much weight as is to be put upon it finally, say some 20,000 tons, and its effects carefully watched and regulated as the loading goes on". He also suggested embanking the terrace to its proposed height before beginning the shaft.[47]

Casey estimated that it would cost $99,102 to accomplish this work, a sum far greater than the $36,000 appropriated by Congress. After carefully weighing all the plans submitted at a meeting on September 25, the commission approved Casey's plan. However, it rejected his request for additional money to complete the foundation. He received specific instructions not to exceed the $36,000 limit. The commission directed him to begin work on October 1.[48]

Although the solution to the foundation was finally decided, attacks against Mills' design continued unabated in Congress and in the Society. The plan for the pantheon at the base of the obelisk—dropped long ago—had never been entirely rejected. However, as time passed and it became obvious that enough money would never be procured, the question of building a pantheon or anything resembling it became purely academic. Most people, whether they liked the Mills design or not, were certain that a pantheon would never be built simply because of the costs. Those opposed to the Mills design at any cost felt that without the pantheon there was greater justification for directing their displeasure at a plain obelisk. Many men of culture agreed that "this form of monument is the refuge of incompetancy in architecture."[49]

The modern architectural critic Ada Louise Huxtable described the basic philosophical differences that lay behind the continuing criticism of the Mills design:

> The Victorian architect based his judgments on a very conscious set of esthetic rules. If he condemned all that was simple, symmetrical, and unadorned, he admired all that was intricate, irregular, and complex. The varied, picturesque outline, with its subtle changes, was considered more 'artful' than regularity. A plain shape or unrelieved surface was 'monotonous' and

Some of the Victorian designs for the completion of the monument. From the left, they are by H. R. Searle, John Frazer, M. P. Hapwood, and Paul Schutze. *Library of Congress (photographs USZ62-4055, USZ62-25575, USZ62-25577, and USZ62-25578, respectively).*

'unimaginative'; infinite and multitudinous variations of form, scale, and ornamentation, preferably of an exotic nature, were the work of creativity. The degree of controlled complication dictated the degree of esthetic success.[50]

Henry van Brunt, a prominent architectural critic of the school of Victorian architects, looked askance at the Mills design. "No person," said he, "interested in our reputation as a civilized people can contemplate this completion without pain." He argued that neither the old design with the pantheon nor the new design without it were adequate for a monument of this nature. He proposed that before the commission commit itself to completing the shaft, it invite architects nationwide to submit designs. He concluded that such an invitation would encourage art in the United States and bring credit to it in "the world of art."[51]

Around the same time that the commission and Congress were listening to Casey's ideas on the foundation, they were also receiving designs from architects and artists all over the country. The commission had not advertised for them, but the furor created by the Mills design prompted architects and artists to send in their ideas in hopes that the commission would consider them. Certainly Congress gave this impression and even encouraged it. Besides, General Humphreys had earlier suggested considering new designs. Most of these designs reflected the Victorian style.

A design drawn by the American sculptor William Wetmore Story, who had his studio in Italy, received special attention. Story proposed to encase the monument with a marble "envelope...profusely enriched, after the manner of the Florentine Gothic of the Campanile of Giotto," and to extend the structure to a height twice the size of the existing stump. He proposed crowning the monument with a pyramid of marble surmounted by a small figure of Fame about 350 feet from the ground.[52]

Story had many friends in Congress who were receptive to his ideas. His plan was especially palatable because he would not raze the partially completed structure. Moreover, some believed, his plan did not require underpinning for the foundation. Many who objected to the Mills design readily accepted Story's. After reviewing the plan, the Joint Committee on Public Buildings and Grounds in Congress asked the Society to study it and render an opinion. At a meeting in December 1878, while Casey was making arrangements to begin work on the foundation, the Society concluded that the Story design was "vastly superior in artistic taste and beauty" to any of the other plans. Because the stump would remain, the Society could justify its about-face by saying that none of the public's past contributions to the monument would be sacrificed. It agreed that the Story plan would "harmonize conflicting opinions and give general satisfaction to the country." The Society recommended the Story plan and appointed a committee of five to confer with committees of Congress on the further prosecution of the work.[53]

Design suggested by William Wetmore Story.
Library of Congress (photograph USZ62-25576).

The Society, acting in an advisory capacity to the Joint Commission, had every right to an opinion on this matter although it was ready to compromise on the design. Confused by the Society's sudden turnabout on the question of design, the commission transmitted the Society's resolution to Congress, asking for instructions on how to proceed.[54] Congress debated the problem of design and the Story plan for more than one year. In the meantime, the commission wisely agreed to continue work on the foundation while Congress debated the issue.[55]

Although the Society as a whole had demonstrated that it was ready to accept the Story plan, not all influential members agreed. Robert C. Winthrop, who as Speaker of the House of Representatives in 1848 gave the major oration at the laying of the monument cornerstone, did not. Although not entirely sympathetic to the Mills design, Winthrop felt that the plan should not be altered because a "whole generation of men, women, and children had contributed, in larger or smaller sums, to this particular monument...." To tear it down to "improve" the design was "abhorrent." His first wish was to complete the monument as a simple obelisk, but if the safety of the foundatin demanded, Story's idea of turning it into an ornamental Lombard Tower was perhaps the best solution.[56]

Robert C. Winthrop.
Library of Congress.

It was one thing to approve the Story concept on an aesthetic basis and another to accept it on practical grounds. When the Building Committee forwarded the design to Casey for his opinion, his reply disappointed many. Casey concluded that, contrary to standing opinion, Story's design would require removal of 41.5 feet of the existing stump to rebuild it with the windows represented in the lower portions of the shaft just above the loggia. Moreover, if Casey followed the Story design without underpinning the existing foundation, the structure would bring pressure on the foundation far too great to sustain the soil underneath. Even if the underpinning ordered by the commission was finished, the total weight imposed by the buttresses and steps of the loggia would still be too great for the improved foundation. Casey concluded that whether the monument was a plain obelisk or Story's ornate design, the foundation would require an underpinning equal to or greater than the one ordered by the Joint Commission.[57]

Casey found this the appropriate time to repeat his request for the $99,102 to complete the foundation. The Joint Commission in turn asked Congress to provide the larger sums so that Casey could restore the foundation in the manner he had suggested. On 27 June 1879, Congress granted Casey's request in a joint resolution that increased the original authorization by $64,000.[58]

When Casey outlined his plan for modifying the foundation to the commission, he also presented his general ideas on the construction of the obelisk. These ideas were obviously not intended to be final because work on the shaft was still a long way off, but Casey felt that in modifying the foundation, he needed to consider the kind of superstructure necessary for such a foundation. Besides, he had already been told by the commission that the shaft would rise to 525 feet:

To carry the monument to the required height..., it is proposed to construct it of masonry to a height of 500 feet, and to crown the shaft with a pyramidal roof of iron, which shall be 25 feet in height. This roof can be covered with hammered glass over some portions, to give light to the well of the monument. The masonry still to be built will be 343 feet 8 inches in height. The walls of the shell will be 8.66 feet in thickness at the bottom; will be vertical on the inside; have a batter of one-quarter of an inch to the foot on the outside; and will be 18 inches in thickness at the top.

For convenience in reference, the new portion of the shaft has been divided into two parts: the lower 172 feet being called the II Division; and the remaining 171 feet 8 inches the I Division. The masonry of the II division will consist of a white marble facing of headers and stretchers, the headers running entirely through the wall, and the stretchers having a bed of at least 2 feet. The quantity of marble to be used in this division will be sufficient to coat the face of the wall 4 feet in thickness. The backing will be of coursed rubble of blue gneiss; the beds and builds of the stones to be dressed to parallel surfaces. All the courses of marble to have 2 feet rise. The walls of the I Division will be built entirely of marble, carefully cut and bonded. Iron cramps and dogs, will be used throughout the construction, and stiffening beams of iron will be let into this masonry at such distances apart as future consideration may show to be necessary. It will be observed that the well for this new portion has not been carried up square but the corners slightly rounded, thus giving additional strength and stiffness in the angles where the faces meet.

The weight of the iron roof will be about thirty tons. The weight of the II Division 13,630 tons, and of the I Division 5,996. The total weight of the finished monument, allowing 220 tons for the stairways, &c., will be 43,671 tons.[59]

Casey had described this plan in July 1878. Although he was especially busy at that time with the foundation, his mind never ceased to consider the obelisk itself.

Meanwhile, George Perkins Marsh, the American Ambassador to Italy, entered the picture. Marsh had extensively studied Egyptian obelisks and was considered an authority on the subject. Writing from Rome in February 1879, Ambassador Marsh described his interest in the monument to Senator George F. Edmunds of Vermont. Edmunds referred Marsh's letter to Casey. Casey wisely listened to Marsh's advice on the construction of the obelisks. They soon became friends, and their acquaintance became the turning point in the completion of the monument.[60]

In his studies Marsh had noted that an obelisk consisted of a naked shaft, with or without inscription. The height was 10 times the width of the base. So, if the base was 50 feet on each side, the height of the shaft had to have been slightly convex, but it was too late to incorporate this feature in the Washington Monument. Marsh believed that the dimensions of the

George Perkins Marsh. *Library of Congress.*

shaft should be reduced as it rose, the top varying from two-thirds to three-quarters of the length of the base.

A major find of Marsh's studies was that the form of the pyramidion was always constant. Its base was exactly the same dimension as the top of the shaft and these were joined together without any break (except for one angle), ledge, or molding. He set the height of the pyramidion at equal to the length of a side of the base of the shaft, and therefore greater than the side of its own base.

Marsh opposed the substitution of a low-hipped roof for an acute pyramidion and adding windows in the face of either the pyramidion or the shaft. He called these elements "attrocities" in the Bunker Hill Monument. However, if the public demanded a window, Marsh felt that it should be the exact size and shape of the ashlar stones of the monument. A close-fitting shutter, the same color as the stone, should be attached to the window.[61]

While Casey and Marsh settled technical design problems, Casey developed another idea to improve the quality of materials. He suggested to the commission that it use coursed granite for the interior walls of the shaft instead of blue gneiss rubble. He believed that granite would provide a much stronger and durable wall and would be cheaper. The commission quickly approved the idea.[62]

With a sure understanding of Marsh's theories, Casey began to put together his plan for completing the superstructure. On 19 April 1880, while work on the foundation was nearing completion, he wrote to Winthrop outlining his design, which had already received the commission's sanction. Casey set the height of the obelisk at 550 feet, with marble facing and granite backing. One hundred and fifty-six feet of the monument had already been completed. Because the base of the shaft was 55 feet on each side, the top would have to be 34.5 feet on each side. The top was to be crowned with a 50-foot pyramidion made of iron and glass. So far, the dimensions conformed to Marsh's theories. Casey then described how he had planned and was strengthening the foundation. He noted that the

$200,000 appropriated by Congress would be exhausted by August 1880, and that it would take $677,000 to complete the monument in four working seasons.[63]

Winthrop leaned toward retaining the existing design. Largely through Casey's efforts, Winthrop was finally convinced that the Society should throw its full weight behind Casey's plan. Spearheading a drive within the Society, Winthrop obtained its approval for Casey's plan. In a letter to Congress, he precisely answered one by one all the criticisms of the modified plan. He argued that the monument:

> was not undertaken to illustrate the fine arts of any period, but to commemorate the foremost man of all the ages.... a simple, sublime shaft, on a very spot selected by Washington himself for a monument of the American Revolution, and rising nearer to the skies than any known monument on earth, will be no unworthy memorial, or inappropriate emblem, of his own exalted character and pre-eminent services.[64]

Former President Hayes, who had delivered the memorable address at the laying of the cornerstone 32 years earlier, was asked to exhort Congress to accept Casey's modified plan. Congress needed little persuasion. It accepted the plan, finally ending the debate over the design. Although criticism continued, Mills' design was vindicated thanks to Casey's modified plan. This victory owed much to Winthrop.[65]

Soon after leaving office, Hayes described his role and that of others in reconciling the serious differences. He wrote that:

> For some months I made it a study—a hobby. General Casey skillfully prepared a plan to strengthen the foundation. Mr. Spofford furnished the height of other tall structures. Mr. Clark, architect of the Capitol, gave constant and indispensable aid to the work. Mr. Corcoran and others earnestly supported the project of going forward, and gradually all opposition was overcome. We decided that the monument should overtop all other structures, and fixed its height, therefore, at 550 feet. On some of the details we consulted our Minister to Italy, Mr. George P. Marsh. Singularly and fortunately he discovered that there was a rule which determined the height of an obelisk by reference to the dimension of its base; and that by the rule our monument should be 550 feet high. ...General Casey is entitled to special and honorable mention. He solved the difficult problem presented by the defective foundation. To him the nation is indebted for the successful completion of its most admirable and illustrious memorial structure.[66]

One of Casey's contemporaries left an interesting account that is not supported by the records. During the debates on whether the existing shaft should be torn down and another design put up in its place, that writer said that the question was referred to a board consisting of General Montgomery

C. Meigs (Quartermaster General of the Army), General Horatio G. Wright (Chief of Engineers succeeding Humphreys), and Colonel William P. Craighill (also of the Corps of Engineers). The board met with President Hayes at the White House. No records were kept of the proceeding and no other persons except Casey were present. The board decided "unanimously that the existing masonry was sufficient and the remaining four hundred feet of the monument was built upon it."[67]

Although meetings in which the advice of various experts was sought were common, this account must remain unsubstantiated. Even though President Hayes and General Wright were members of the Joint Commission, it is difficult to believe that they would have acted without the concurrence of the whole commission. Moreover, even though Hayes took an active part at meetings of the commission, he gave equal credit for the monument's completion to individual members of the commission, including Corcoran, Clark, and Hill, who were not present at the alleged meeting.

The years 1876-1880 were trying ones for the monument project. Disagreements and criticisms, sometimes bordering on hostility, ran rampant in Congress, the Society, and artistic circles. The Joint Commission, a congressionally appointed body responsible to Congress alone, was in a difficult position. Delegated by law to achieve the best possible design while being economical, the commission was responsible to a body that was in itself divided over the design. It therefore had to maneuver carefully and diplomatically to avoid accusations of partisanship. In Casey the commission was fortunate to have an honest and first-rate engineer in whom it had the utmost faith and confidence. Casey must receive the credit for finding a solution to ensure the foundation's safety and achieve the Mills design.

Casey fortunately had the assistance of Ambassador Marsh, who provided the technical theory needed to formulate the modified design; Winthrop and President Hayes, who lent their moral support in Congress and elsewhere; and his colleagues Davis and later Green who helped in the arduous task of the day-to-day affairs of construction.

Chapter V

THE MONUMENT RISES

Preparations

In October 1878, after the Joint Commission told Casey to begin work on the foundation, he immediately started construction. Many things remained to be done before he could begin. Old supply shelters and workshops that could still be used needed repair, and new ones had to be built. Several of the old facilities that had fallen into decay had been removed in 1875. Tools and machinery, particularly derricks needed to hoist the heavy stone, had to be procured and assembled. A variety of materials such as marble, granite, cement, and iron, had to be purchased by contract. Casey lost much work time advertising for proposals, awarding contracts, and waiting for delivery of supplies.

Casey and Davis had to recruit a sizeable labor force with a variety of skills. They had trouble finding skilled workers, who were much sought after in Washington. Some workers came from nearby Baltimore, which was close to the quarries. Despite this source, construction managers had to recruit workers from as far away as New England.

In early October the commission gave Casey $3,000 to repair existing structures and to build carpenter, rigger, blacksmith, and stonecutter shops and a cement stone house. By the end of the month workers completed most of these temporary facilities. They reroofed the old one-story lapidarium, which had been used for storing the memorial stones for many years, and replastered the two small rooms at the ends of this structure for administrative purposes.[1]

Casey furnished the blacksmith shop with three forges and a supply of tools and other necessary materials. A new road connecting the monument grounds to 14th Street helped move supplies. Although the lumber for the stonecutter shed was delivered early, it was not built until the following year because work on the shaft would not begin for a long time. When completed, the shed measured 76 by 36 feet.[2]

Casey anticipated that work on the shaft would require an even larger labor force. In January 1880 he requested more stonecutter sheds, railroad tracks about the monument grounds to help in receiving and handling heavy supplies, a safety net at the top of the shaft to prevent accidents, and a latrine for the workmen. He proposed using the western end of the cement house as an additional blacksmith shop. Although work on the obelisk was several months away, it was typical of Casey to plan well in advance. The commission allowed Casey to build these and other facilities.[3]

To improve safety conditions around the base of the foundation, Casey ordered all debris from the old construction work removed from the top of the shaft. Workmen placed new blocks, faces, and supports in position to permit access to the top and installed new wooden doors at the base to prevent entry by vandals and unauthorized people. Accumulated debris in the well at the center of the foundation was also removed to 23 feet. To measure any settlement of the shaft, a bench mark was cut at the top of each of the corners of the fourth step of the foundation, counting from the bottom. Each bench mark was compared and made to correspond exactly in height.[4]

Although Casey left a wealth of detail about the methods and machinery he used, little has been published on the subject. Work on the monument required basically two different types of operations—digging around and beneath the foundation and lifting very heavy loads to high altitudes and setting them into place on the shaft. The equipment used to strengthen the foundation was generally common for its day, but the work was burdensome and delicate. The workmen had to remove huge quantities of earth from underneath and around the foundation without disturbing the earth supporting it. Casey used three basic types of machines. Derricks, concrete mixers, and hoisting equipment removed and carried earth to the surface and mixed and carried concrete to the bottom to form the foundation. By the end of 1878, four derricks and two concrete mixers run by steam engines were positioned around the base of the shaft. About 580 feet of 4-inch vitrified pipes drained the water from the concrete mixers. Casey also ordered cars, sling bodies, and tubs built to remove the earth from cuts and transport the concrete to fill the excavations. These cars ran on a network of iron rails.[5]

In September 1878 Casey wrote to a correspondent who asked how he would build the shaft: "It is impossible now to furnish drawings showing plan...but I would say in general terms that machinery will be required capable of raising weights of 10,000 pounds to the height of 500 feet and the engine should be so constructed that its power could be used for other purposes than hoisting." He concluded that it would be desirable to use an engine that could not only hoist extremely heavy stones and workmen to unusual heights, but that could also lift a passenger elevator in the completed monument.[6] Casey was seeking equipment that could serve two purposes: first as a tool in the construction of the monument, and later as a permanent facility to serve visitors.

Casey's plan required a large quantity of iron to form a skeletal

Workmen hoist a piece of marble with the help of a stone-setting crane atop the monument. *Library of Congress (photograph USZ62-15293).*

framework rising almost the full height of the monument. A temporary platform elevator run by a permanently installed passenger elevator engine would lift the stones and other supplies inside the shaft. Four wooden cranes swung from Phoenix iron columns that supported a permanent stairway would set the stones.[7] Because Casey had planned for a permanent facility, it required the commission's approval, which was quickly granted.[8]

The plan required a pit 16.5 feet long, 10 feet wide, and 7.83 feet deep in the floor of the obelisk. A winding drum, inserted in the pit, would hold the hoisting ropes. The Phoenix columns of the elevator and stairway also went into the pit. The workers completed it the end of 1879.[9]

Workmen constructed a scaffold or platform inside the top of the shaft, where they placed a derrick to receive the stone and remove the deteriorated courses of marble and other debris.[10] This was done without the elevator, which had yet to be constructed.

Casey knew that progress depended upon the timely delivery of supplies. Unfortunately, no matter how carefully he selected contractors or how adamantly he insisted on the timely arrival and acceptable condition of supplies, items were frequently late. Those that did arrive on time were sometimes inadequate. This was especially true of marble, an item that, if not quarried or dressed properly, could mar the beauty of a structure or even weaken it. Late deliveries were not always the fault of the contractors. Sometimes strikes, weather, transportation, or other unforseen events slowed shipments. Regardless of the reason, Casey showed little sympathy for contractors who did not meet their obligations.

The company that provided Portland cement caused costly delays. Casey had selected J.B. White and Brothers, a New York firm, because he considered their Portland cement the strongest and best known in Europe and America. He was deeply disappointed when, for one reason or another, the contractor repeatedly failed to make his deliveries. With no cement to make concrete, Casey was forced to lay off workers. This strained his plans and projections. After several of these costly delays, Captain Davis wrote the contractor that "past and prospective failure to keep up this supply make your execution of the contract anything but satisfactory."[11]

Contracts for purchasing marble presented the most serious problems. Casey took great pains to see that the marble he bought matched that on the unfinished obelisk and that it was the most durable of its kind. His specifications to prospective bidders were clear:

> The marble must be white, strong, sound, and free from flint, shakes, powder cracks, or seams, and must in texture and color so conform to the marble now built in the monument as not to present any marked or striking contrast in color, lustre, or shade, when set in the wall.
> The stock must also be free from impurities that would so discolor the stone as to deface the general appearance of the work to a greater extent than that now shown in the portion of the monument erected.... each bid must be accompanied by a slab of the marble, sawed or fine cut perpendicular to the quarry bed.... These cubes when subjected to a crushing pressure between steel plates with cushions of wood, must sustain a pressure of at least 8000 lbs. to the square inch.
> If the bidder has a chemical analysis of his stock he will submit an authenticated copy of the same with his proposal.[12]

At the end of 1878 Casey tested several specimens of marble from the unfinished structure and from the Baltimore County, Maryland, quarries where the old marble had been obtained for strength and durability. The two-inch cubes were crushed in the Corps' New York office by a hydrostatic press. The 12 specimens from the top of the shaft compared favorably with crystal marble specimens from the quarries.[13]

On 19 July 1879, Casey invited proposals for bids on rough marble.

To make an intelligent selection of contractors, Casey ordered Davis to inspect the quarries of four bidders in New England, New York, and Baltimore to determine whether their facilities could produce the desired quantity of marble. Davis reported that John A. Briggs' quarry in Sheffield, Massachusetts, could supply the amount needed. Moreover, Davis felt that this marble's color and texture would not significantly contrast with the marble already in place. Based on Davis' conclusions, Briggs received a contract for 12,000 cubic feet of rough marble.[14]

Before long Casey realized his mistake in selecting Briggs. The company repeatedly failed to make timely deliveries, and when the marble came, the dimensions were incorrect and the stone defective in color. Casey and his assistant rejected many of these pieces, but their careful scrutiny caused delays.[15] After acquiring enough marble to cover an area on the monument six feet high, Casey annulled the contract in July 1880. During the same month, he signed a contract with Hugh Sisson of Baltimore for 40,000 cubic feet of white marble from his quarry in Beaver Dam in Baltimore County, the same general area from which the marble for the unfinished shaft had come.[16]

Although a much more reliable contractor than Briggs, Sisson also had his faults. Casey relied heavily on Sisson's continuing ability to quarry marble, even during moderate winter weather, because of his excellent equipment and facilities. Still there were delays in delivery, with the consequent lay-off of marble cutters and laborers. These delays became so serious that at one point the Joint Committee felt compelled to annul the contract. Casey was the first to admit that Sisson had violated his contract, but he was convinced that the contractor was doing the best he could to produce the necessary quantity of marble. Casey recommended to the commission that the contract not be annulled, pointing out that it would be difficult to get a more reliable contractor unless the contract called for the delivery of all the marble needed to complete the monument at one time. Because annual congressional appropriations were limited, such a stipulation would be impossible.[17]

Thanks to Casey, Sisson continued to supply marble through succeeding contracts signed in May 1881 and May 1882. However, in April 1883 the Joint Commission considered a contract with the Lee Marble Company, a New York firm with quarries in Lee, Massachusetts. This company's price of $1.29 a cubic foot outbid Sisson's price of $1.50. Although Casey had some reservations as to the company's ability to quarry marble during winter months, the quality of the marble and the fairness of the price impressed him. Based on Casey's recommendation, the commission took on the new contract.

Casey soon found he had made another mistake. After Casey granted the company four extensions for the initial delivery and Davis visited the quarry to determine its ability to fulfill its agreement, the Lee

Marble Company requested that its contract be annulled.[18] The commission agreed and immediately signed a contract with its old supplier, Hugh Sisson. Rough marble soon began to arrive at the monument site, but Casey had lost three months of work.[19]

Working with marble presented some unique problems. Because the stone could be easily damaged or defaced while being quarried, it could only be removed carefully and at considerable expense. Slight discolorations and cracks in pieces of marble, however minor, could easily affect the beauty of the finished structure. Careful inspections at the site delayed the construction of the monument despite Casey's planning.

Contracts for building materials like granite and iron did not present such serious problems, although Casey was equally adamant in his demands that these items be of the highest quality. His specifications to bidders for rough granite were as precise as those for marble:

> the granite must be strong, sound, and [free] from shakes, powder cracks or seams, but it is not required that it should be free from stains, unless these are due to some foreign impurities that will cause the disintegration of the stone.... each bid must be accompanied by three (3) cubes dressed accurately.... These cubes when subjected to a crushing pressure between steel plates with cushions of wood, must sustain a pressure of at least 16,000 lbs. per square inch.... Bidders must be able to show to the contracting agent of the United States, that they have quarries and sufficient 'plant' in place, in such working order as to be able to comply with these specifications and to furnish the stock as desired.[20]

All the granite came from several Maine suppliers. It arrived at the monument site with almost no difficulty. A durable stone, the granite was not subject to the same scrutiny as the marble because it was used for the interior of the shaft. There was always an adequate supply of granite, even during the winter, so the stonecutters could even work through the winter.[21]

Iron, another major item, also presented few contract problems. In late 1879, while preparing for work on the shaft, the commission contracted for the delivery of enough iron to construct the stairway and elevator shaft to 250 feet.[22]

When Casey took charge of the monument's construction in July 1878, he supervised not only his assistant Captain Davis, one clerk, and one draftsman, but a labor force of six riggers, one mason, three stonecutters, two drillers, two carpenters, 26 laborers, one night watchman, and one water boy. With the exception of Davis, this crew accounted for total wages of $504.79, modest even for those days.[23] Casey used this force largely to clean up the area, help form plans, and in general prepare for the construction. More men would be needed once work on the foundation and the obelisk began.

Casey conducted his own recruiting. Experience taught him that it took advanced planning to recruit skilled and experienced workers of the kind needed for the monument. In September 1878 he wrote to the chief engineer of the Sutro Tunnel in Virginia City, Nevada, that to underpin the monument he needed skilled workmen accustomed to subterraneous excavations and the accompanying great pressures. "Men," he said, "whom I would be willing to trust for this work are not to be found here." But, he added, "it has occurred to me I might find them among the mines in Nevada who have had much experience in tunneling through enormous clay deposits which are so extensive all through the Comstock." Casey wanted one or two men with this experience and skill to supervise others, "men who do not mind the mud, darkness, and danger of such working."[24]

Whether anything came of this request is uncertain, but it does indicate how important Casey considered this work. That same month Casey visited Baltimore where workmen were tunneling and excavating for a water supply system. He found a few skillful men there to oversee excavations on the monument's foundation.[25]

By the beginning of 1879, when work on the foundation was well underway, the labor force had more than doubled and wages had reached $2,785.61. The addition of several skilled workers was responsible for some of this increase in the payroll. Seven months later the work force reached 175 men, most of whom were working on the foundation.[26]

The monument in August of 1879 with work on the foundation in progress. The pond behind the monument is Babcock Lake, which was later drained and filled to protect the foundation's stability. *Library of Congress (photograph USZ62-10828).*

As work on the shaft was ready to begin in 1880, Casey began to calculate how many stonecutters he would need in relation to the amount of marble and granite that would be delivered during the first year. Assuming that one stonecutter could prepare six cubic feet of stone in one day, Casey estimated it would require 120 stonecutters to dress stone in 4.5 months. If he employed 120 stonecutters, he would need 5,000 cubic feet each of marble and granite each month. He would also need additional sheds, blacksmith forges, and other related facilities to accommodate such a large work force.[27]

Most of the labor force consisted of marble and granite stonecutters. In July 1880 there were only 40 cutters on the payroll, but by the end of the following month there were 62. This number increased steadily until it passed 100.[28]

While Casey recruited stonecutters, he was beseiged by applicants who were sponsored by congressmen. Because the quantity of stone was below expected levels and adequate work and housing facilities were not available, Casey had to turn away many of them. Davis wrote to one congressman from Maine that "if you send a list of names of men whom you have recommended, they will be entered on our list and sent for as rapidly as vacancies occur for them and they can be given work."[30]

At the peak of construction, the work force reached approximately 170. This number varied as the situation changed. The crew consisted of marble and granite cutters, stone setters or masons, blacksmiths, carpenters, riggers, engine drivers, machinists, firemen, water and tool boys, and ordinary laborers. Next to stonecutters, laborers comprised the largest group. Casey spent about $8,500 a month on wages for this sizeable force.[30]

Casey hired marble cutters on the assumption that the marble would be delivered on time and in the desired quantities. Because this was often not the case, marble cutters were either furloughed or worked only part time. This situation led the marble cutters to petition the commission to reduce their 10-hour day to eight. Casey agreed because he felt it would not affect construction. In arguing the cutter's case before the Building Committee, he pointed out that there would be no increased cost to the United States because the cutters' work was done entirely by the "piece or so much per square foot of cutting accomplished." Casey had one reservation, however—that the arrangement might cause friction with those workers who still had to work 10 hours a day. The idea was accepted by the Building Committee with the stipulation that if the amount of marble delivered increased or if ill feelings developed among the labor force, Casey would have to return to the 10-hour day. It is not known how long this plan remained in effect, but it was to be only a temporary measure until marble deliveries picked up.[31]

Casey did not have these problems with the granite cutters. Because deliveries were usually substantial, the crew constantly worked fulltime. A comparison of wages during the second phase of construction with wages paid for the same set of skills during the first stage (1848 and 1854) reveals only a modest change. Those who benefited during these years were the stonecutters, whose growing national union had made large inroads in the construction industry. In 1880, both marble and granite stonecutters and stonemasons received $2.50 a day. By 1884 marble cutters received $3.50 a day. Compared to wages earned in 1851 this was a modest increase, but compared to other skills, it was substantial. The ordinary laborer did not fare as well as the skilled worker. In 1879 laborers were classified into three categories: a first class laborer earned $1.75 a day; a second class laborer $1.50; and a third class laborer $1.25. Compared with the $1.00 a day earned by laborers three decades earlier, wages had not gone up perceptibly.[32]

Casey demonstrated a sincere concern for the welfare of his workers, recognizing the dangers and tediousness of the job. Before work started on the shaft, he built a safety net around the four sides of the top of the obelisk, which saved several lives. While Casey was in charge of the monument work, no one died because of an accident.[33]

Casey also appreciated excellent work. In 1884 he recommended to the Building Committee that his overseer, P.H. McLaughlin, receive an increase of $25 in his monthly wage. In November 1884, as the obelisk approached completion, Casey extended his generosity to the men working at the top of the structure by offering them coffee in "moderate quantities" to overcome the bitter cold.[34]

Casey had little tolerance for work stoppages. Striking longshoremen in New York prevented the delivery of Portland cement for the foundation, which deeply annoyed him. Later when the monument was nearly complete, strikes were fairly common at the site, particularly among stonecutters, who had a strong union. In September 1884, during one of these strikes, Davis frantically telegraphed Casey, who was in New Hampshire at the time:

> Another strike: Man discharged for carelessly spoiling stone; he denies carelessness asserting blind seam. I investigated minutely. Satisfied cutter was at fault and declined to pay him for four days work done. All hands quit until man was paid. I replied that you would decide on returning to city regarding equity of claim of man discharged. They still declined to resume until man was paid. Gen. Newton approves my course but prefers to take no action in your absence. Suggests that I telegraph facts to you. He would close the sheds rather than submit to bull dozing. Value of stone spoiled seventy five dollars....[35]

Underpinning the Foundation

Freezing weather delayed excavation work, but by the end of January 1879, Casey had enough facilities, machinery, tools, supplies, and workmen on hand to begin underpinning the foundation. The original foundation, constructed in 1848, consisted of a rubble masonry of blue gneiss laid in lime mortar. The foundation measured 80 feet at the base on each of its four sides, 58.5 feet at the top, and 23.5 feet high. The footings were 7.67 feet below the surface. The foundation, which rested on a loam composed of equal parts of sand and clay, weighed about 32,000 long tons. Some small boulders were interspersed throughout the earth. The permanent water level was 12.5 feet below the footings.[36]

Excavation in preparation for pouring concrete beneath the old foundation. *Library of Congress (photograph USZ62-30613).*

Casey developed a two-step plan to strengthen the foundation. Both stages called for widening and deepening the existing foundation to distribute the weight of the monument over a larger area. During the first stage, workmen would place a mass of concrete 13.5 feet thick below the foundation, which would extend 23 feet outward beyond its edge. The second step involved removing a portion of the old foundation from beneath the shaft and placing buttresses in each of the four corners and one in the center of each side. These buttresses were to be extended to make contact with the new slab.[37] The first step removed 10,334 cubic yards, or 70 percent of the earth, under the old foundation and replaced it with a huge concrete slab. This slab extended the foundation on each of its four sides to 126.5 feet, which enlarged the area covered from the original 6,400 square feet to nearly 16,000 square feet. The whole mass contained 7,003 cubic yards of concrete, a mixture consisting of one part Portland cement, two parts sand, three parts pebbles, and four parts broken stone. After this concrete set for 7.5 months, it would have a crushing strength of 155 tons per square foot.[38]

The first phase of construction, begun on 10 February 1879, and completed without any serious problems on November 1, would have been completed sooner except for delays in the shipment of Portland cement. The second phase, the construction of the buttresses, began in September 1879. Immediately after work started, Casey told the Building Committee that he wanted to modify this part of his original plan. He had proposed cross walls, or a leg of masonry concrete, under the center of the foundation, but now he suggested that the earth remain undisturbed "as there could be no lateral displacement of it, and it would yield but an insignificant degree under its present load." He also proposed building a "continuing" concrete buttress to support the foundation and unite the old and the new foundation instead of putting three buttresses on each side as he originally suggested. The new idea was quickly approved by the committee and adopted by the commission.[39]

Sections of the old foundation are removed to make way for construction of concrete buttresses, October 1879. *Library of Congress (photograph USZ62-26189).*

On 28 May 1880, the crew completed the second stage of underpinning. The concrete that went into the buttresses consisted of one part Portland cement, one and one-half parts sand, two and one-quarter parts pebbles, and three parts broken stone. Casey wanted the concrete for the buttresses to be much stronger than the concrete used for the slab. Workmen excavated approximately 348 cubic yards from the old foundation and used about 520 cubic yards of cement for the buttresses.[40]

On June 7 Casey's men began covering the new foundation with the earth that had been excavated. In five weeks they completed the embankment that provided a terrace all around the shaft. The embankment was 30

Buttresses on southeast side of the monument, January 1880. *Library of Congress (photograph USZ62-30612).*

feet wide and 17 feet above the general level of the site. In December Casey recommended to the Building Committee that they extend the terrace another 30 feet by using the old blue stone that had been dug up during the underpinning. He believed that because this refuse was heavier than ordinary earth, it would lend greater support to the foundation. The committee approved his proposal, and contract workers completed the job the following year. When enlarged, the embankment was 175 feet on each side "on the edge of the crest" and 220 feet at the foot of the slopes. The embankment contained 11,810 cubic yards of dirt and gneiss rock.[41] With the embankment finished, work on the foundation was essentially completed.

Casey's plan for strengthening and underpinning the foundation was not new to engineers of his day. What was new was his ability to accomplish such a delicate operation on such a large scale. Although some criticized his plan long after it was executed, particularly pessimists who claimed that the new foundation would never support the completed monument, it received world-wide acclaim.

New foundation completed in May 1880. *Library of Congress (photograph USZ62-15294).*

Casey described his work on the foundation at the monument's dedication in 1885:

> As completed, the new foundation covers two and a half times as much area and extends thirteen and a half feet deeper than the old one. Indeed, the bottom of the new work is only two feet above the level of high tides in the Potomac, while the water which permeates the earth of the monument lot, stands six inches above this bottom. The foundation now rests upon a bed of fine sand some two feet in thickness, and this sand stratum rests upon a bed of boulders and gravel. Borings have been made in this gravel deposit for a depth of over 18 feet without passing through it, and so uniform is the character of the material upon which the foundation rests that the settlements of several corners of the shaft have differed from each other by only the smallest subdivision of an inch. The pressures on the earth beneath the foundation are nowhere greater than the experience of years have shown this earth to be able to sustain, while the strength of the masonry in the foundation itself is largely in excess of the strains brought upon it. The stability of this base is assured against all natural causes except earthquakes or the washing out of the sand bed beneath the foundation.[42]

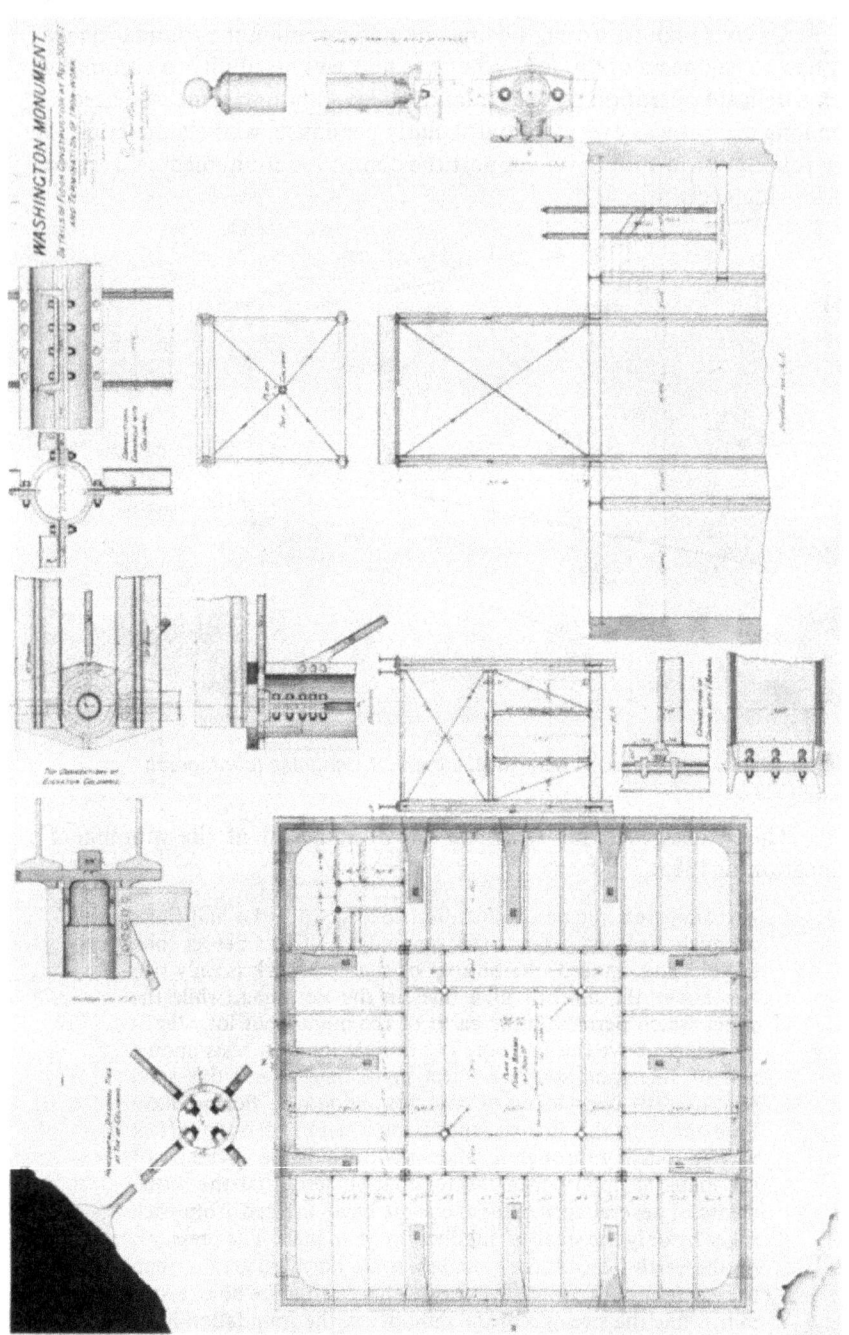

Diagrams of floor construction at the top of the monument and the ironwork for stairs and floor. *National Archives (Record Group 79, file 74.4-26).*

The underpinning had been finished without the slightest crack or damage to any part of the completed shaft. What may have pleased Congress even more was that the new foundation cost $94,474, well within Casey's estimate and the two appropriations voted by Congress.[43]

The Obelisk

After completing the new foundation, Casey and his assistants reorganized the work force and rearranged the machinery and plant to begin work on raising the obelisk to 555 feet. While work continued on the foundation, workers placed derricks atop the shaft. Meanwhile 380 feet of stone sheds were added to the 76 feet already built. A railroad network of 2,600 feet was laid and equipped with turntables and cars to help move heavy supplies to and from the main railroad line and the monument site.[44]

Two basic materials, stone (marble and granite) and iron, comprised the obelisk. Casey used iron to build the elevator and skeletal framework. He started construction on both early because they had to be installed before work could begin on raising the shaft.

In June 1879 Casey presented his construction plan to the commission. Unfortunately, he had not found in the Society's old records any indication of the technique used to hoist stones to the top of the obelisk. It was obvious from existing conditions that the plan had been to construct a stairway in the well of the shaft, but how was not clear. The positions of the donated memorial stones convinced Casey that the original builders had intended for the east and west faces of the shaft to sustain the landings of the staircase, while the north and south faces would bear the staircases and steps. Casey decided to follow this arrangement for the staircase.

The steps and landings, which were to be made of wrought and cast iron, measured 56 inches wide. The sum of the rise and tread of the steps was a little more than 17.75 inches. The well of the stairway was to be 15.75 feet on each side. The I beams and channel bars that formed the platforms and stairway carriages would be strongly fastened into wrought iron Phoenix columns set on each corner of the well. All the coverings and ceilings of the platforms, treads, and rises of the steps were to be cast iron.[45]

Casey planned to set smaller wrought iron Phoenix columns within the staircase well. These columns were then to be connected by bars and braces to the large Phoenix columns that supported the staircase and to the I beams of the landings. All eight Phoenix columns and the I beams of the platforms were to be extended above the top of the obelisk as work progressed. This would establish points of support for the hoisting machinery of the elevator platform and supply the vertical support for the revolving arms of derricks used in setting the masonry upon the shaft.

Casey proposed to run the elevator with an engine powerful enough to raise the heaviest load 50 feet per minute. He estimated that he needed nearly 550 tons of iron to build the staircase and elevator shaft. During the first year he needed enough iron to raise the monument to 250 feet. The Joint Commission approved Casey's plan the same month that he submitted it.[46]

Casey described his idea of an elevator car to prospective contractors. The car would operate within the four small Phoenix columns that formed the elevator shaft, which enclosed a square space just over 9.75 feet on each side. Excluding the car, the greatest weight the elevator was expected to carry was six tons.

Two hoisting ropes were to pull the car, made of the best annealed iron wire or steel, each would have a tensile strength sufficient to raise the heaviest load. The winding drum would be located on the floor of the obelisk's well. Shafting and a train of cog wheels would transmit the power. The engine and boiler to produce the power would be outside the west face of the monument and level with the top of the foundation. The winding drum would hold 500 feet of rope.[47]

With his plan approved by the commission, Casey moved quickly. In August he signed a contract with the Phoenix Iron Company of Trenton, New Jersey, to supply a 250-foot-tall iron framework. In November he issued a contract to Otis Brothers and Company of New York City to produce the elevator and its hoisting machinery.[48] That same month Casey's men completed the pit to house the winding drum. It measured 16.5 feet long, 10 feet wide, and 7.82 feet deep. The walls, cast in one piece, were made of the same concrete mixture used in making the foundation buttresses. Workers also placed the four granite blocks that would encase the foot plates of the Phoenix columns of the staircase. The crew excavated the holes in the interior walls to receive the I beams and channel bars, with mortice holes ranging from 8 to 24 inches in depth.[49]

After the mortice holes were completed, the Phoenix Iron Company immediately began setting the iron framework into place. By the end of January 1880, the framework reached 40 feet, and by the middle of March it rose to 180 feet. Otis Brothers began work on the elevator on 1 April and finished by 12 July. Casey immediately tested and accepted the elevator, winding drum, engine, and boiler. At the same time, Casey's men prepared the equipment to lift and set the large blocks of stone on top of the obelisk. They finished by mid-July.[50]

When Casey took charge of construction, the monument was already 156 feet high. The top courses installed during the period of Know-Nothing control had been put up with the "refuse" pieces of marble scattered about the site. The headers of several pieces of marble in these courses were too small to be used in Casey's plan. Also, the marble facing at the top had been forced slightly outward for some distance downward, probably by the expansion of frozen water that had gotten in between the backing and facing. Casey recommended that 6 feet of marble be removed from the top and that

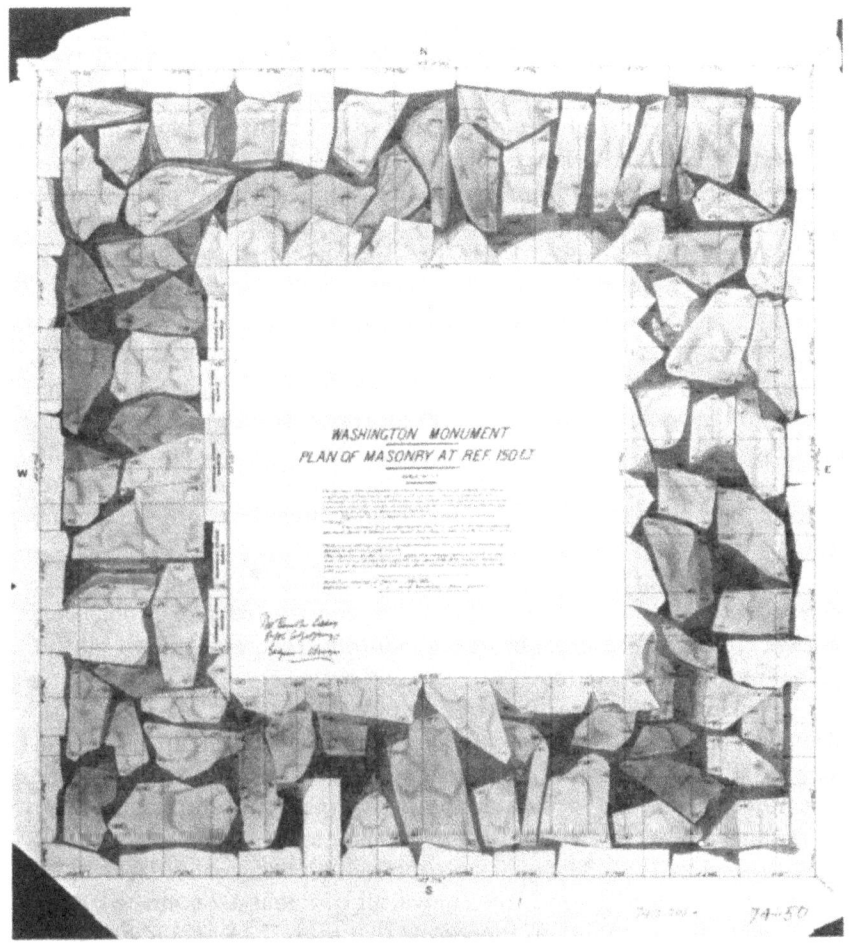

After removing six feet of damaged marble, Casey reinforced the deteriorated mortar between the stones beneath. The dark areas in this cross section view from the top represent cavities between the stones, cleared of old mortar and refilled with hydraulic cement. The diagram shows the blue gneiss stones in the interior, the marble face of the monument, and the memorial stones in the interior shaft. *National Archives (Record Group 79, file 74.2-203).*

the wall be reset with new marble, thereby giving it the diminished thickness his plan demanded.

He strongly believed that these actions would have several advantages. For one thing, after eliminating 6 feet he could secure a stronger masonry by reaching a section of mortar less disintegrated from the effects of the frost. For another, he could secure a rectangular figure to begin work that was less distorted from a square than the edges of the courses above 150 feet. Finally, Casey would be able to begin the sloping masonry of the inside well at the bottom of a flight of stairs. This would secure a uniform increase in the dimensions of the stairway rising from the 150-foot to the 160-foot platform, at which point the new dimensions of the well would begin.[51]

The commission approved Casey's recommendations, and by mid-July his men began to remove three courses (6 feet high) of the old marble. They then prepared the surface of the 150-foot level to receive the new stone by removing the spalls and disintegrated mortar that lay between the granite and marble pieces and filling the voids with hydraulic cement concrete. These fillings varied in depth from a few inches to several feet.[52] The work was completed within two weeks.

The corner stone was laid on Saturday, August 7, amid fanfare that marked the resumption of work on the monument. President and Mrs. Hayes, Dr. Joseph M. Toner, a distinguished member of the Society, the secretary of the Joint Commission, Captain Davis, and Casey attended the ceremony. The new elevator raised them all to the 150-foot level. Before the stone was lowered and set in place, President Hayes placed a small coin, with his initials and the month, day, and year scratched in it, in the cement bed.[53]

By the end of 1880, Casey's crew had added 22 feet to the shaft, which now reached 172 feet. They also constructed a 20-foot iron framework, which they brought to the 200-foot level, and shifted all the hoisting machinery to the top.[54]

Work on the shaft progressed as rapidly as possible. The speed with which the obelisk rose depended largely on the arrival of materials. As usual, shipping delays, particularly of marble, frustrated Casey, who had all his moves planned. However disappointing these slowdowns may have been at times, Casey had enough stone on hand to raise the obelisk to 250 feet by the end of 1881. The quarries supplied an average of 103 blocks of marble a month through 1881, the equivalent of about 3.2 courses, or 6.4 feet, added to the height in one month. At that rate, 77 feet could be added to the height of the shaft each year. Therefore Casey estimated it would take three more seasons to complete the monument.[55]

At the end of each November, Casey gave the commission a list of his expenditures. He always indicated how far the balance would go towards the monument and how much more he needed to complete it. He stressed that if Congress did not pass its appropriation in time, work would have to stop. Fortunately, Congress usually provided the sums he asked for. By the end of 1881, in addition to the $200,000 provided in the act of 1876, Congress had passed two appropriations totalling $300,000. At that time Casey still had $61,257, which would have taken him as far as June 1882. He estimated that he needed another $200,000 to continue the work through fiscal 1883.

Although Casey requested $200,000 at the end of 1881, he received only $150,000 in the last appropriation. By the end of 1882, he had a balance of $33,417 after expenditures. When Casey submitted his 1882 report to the commission, he estimated he would need another $250,000 to finish the shaft, pyramidion, staircase, and elevator.

In 1882 the marble arrived from the quarries in greater quantities than expected, so by the end of November an additional 90 feet of stone was added to the shaft. The obelisk now reached 340 feet. Casey estimated that the walls of the shaft and pyramidion would be completed by mid-1884.[58]

Casey's design called for the proportion of granite backing to the marble facing to diminish as the walls rose. When the obelisk reached 450 feet, the granite backing would stop and the walls from there to the summit would be entirely of marble.

Although 1882 was a relatively good year for the delivery of marble, 1883 was not. Up to that time Hugh Sisson provided all the marble, except for the brief interval of the Massachusetts Marble Company contract. In 1883, however, the selection of the Lee Marble Company of New York led to the loss of three months of work because the company failed to fulfill its contract. As a result, in 1883 the workmen added only 70 feet to the obelisk, making it 410 feet tall.[59]

The monument nearing completion in 1882, seen from the White House lawn. *Library of Congress (photograph USZ62-24664).*

By the end of 1883, the stone masons finished dressing the last of the granite backing. Casey revised his earlier estimate. He believed that enough marble was arriving to enable completion of both the walls and pyramidion by the end of the 1884 working season.[60]

In the meantime, Congress appropriated the $250,000 that Casey had requested the previous year. With the balance of the 1882 appropriation, $153,375 remained. Casey felt this was sufficient to finish the walls of the shaft, the pyramidion, staircase and platforms, floor, and elevator. This estimate did not include the embellishment of the doors, construction of the terrace or approaches to the monument, insertion of the memorial stones, or installation of a lighting system in the interior of the monument.[61]

On 9 August 1884, the masons set the last piece of marble in place, completing the shaft to 500 feet. Due to the thinness of the walls at this height, the stonemasons took extreme care in setting these stones. Between the 440th and 452nd levels, they freely used galvanized iron clamps. Between the 452nd and 500th-foot levels, they set the walls entirely of marble. Beginning at the 470-foot level, where the ribs of the pyramidion began, mortises and tenons cut in the builds and beds of the marble secured the courses of marble together.[62] Only the construction of the pyramidion remained.

The Pyramidion

When Casey presented his plan for completing the obelisk to the Joint Commission in 1878, he described a pyramidal roof of metal and hammered glass to provide light for the interior. He had fixed the height of the pyramidion at 25 feet.[63] Since those early years, however, he had strengthened the foundation and modified the shaft. Following the theories of Ambassador Marsh, he heightened the monument to 555 feet and lengthened the pyramidion to 55 feet. The walls of the obelisk became thinner the higher they rose, thereby placing as little weight as possible on the foundation. Weight, therefore, became a significant factor in developing his plans for the obelisk.

As the walls of the shaft neared completion, Casey and civil engineer Bernard Richardson Green, a long-time member of Casey's staff, decided a metal roof would be too heavy for the monument. They also agreed that if metal or some other materials employed on the roof were different from the marble walls, they would probably discolor and ruin the white marble. In short, the roof was to be of the same marble as the walls, cut in slabs that were as large as possible to reduce the number of joints.

Green was born on 28 December 1843, in Malden, Massachusetts. He began his engineering career as a civilian with the Corps of Engineers. For 14 years he worked primarily on the construction of coastal defenses in the northeast. It was on these assignments during the Civil War that he met Casey.

When Casey assumed responsibility for the Office of Public Buildings and Grounds in 1877, he had Green transferred to Washington to work

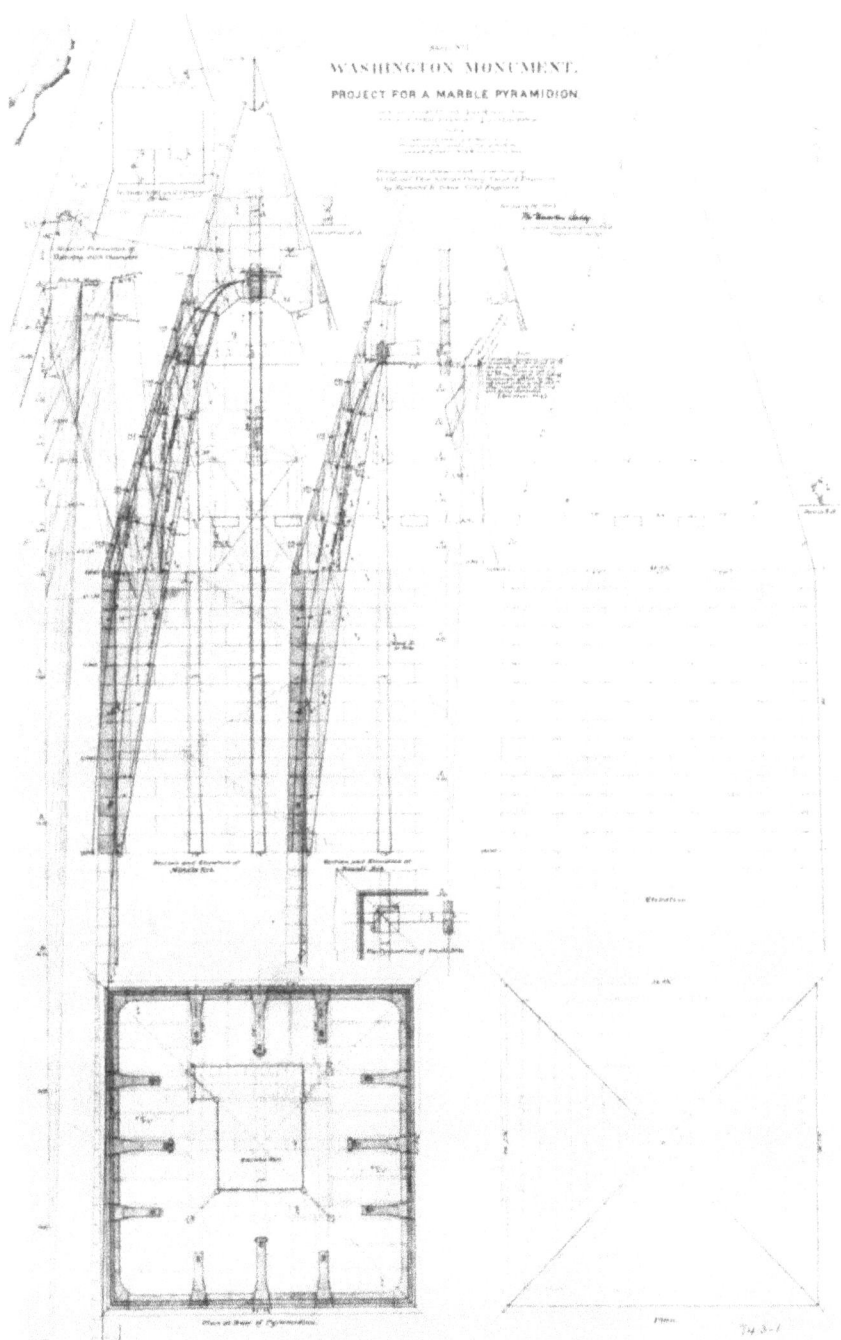

These detailed diagrams of the pyramidion by Bernard Richardson Green show the exterior and interior of the monument, ironwork of the decks, stairs and elevator and calculations on stability and stress. *National Archives (Record Group 79, file 74.3-1).*

under him. Green distinguished himself as an architectural engineer during the construction of many government buildings. After Casey's assignment to the Washington National Monument, he entrusted Green with the completion of the State, War, and Navy Building. Green introduced new construction methods and because of his efficient management the structure was completed at a much smaller cost than originally estimated.

Green also supervised the construction of the Army Medical Museum and of some of the principal buildings of the Soldiers Home. After Casey resigned as engineer in charge of the monument in 1888, Green worked under him at the new Library of Congress. When Casey died in 1896, Green was appointed in his place. After the Library was completed in 1897, he was made its superintendent, an office he held until his death. During the years he held this position, his interest in the Washington National Monument never ceased. He often gave advice on how best to maintain the monument in a sound condition.[64]

Before 1881 Green's name does not appear often in the monument's official records. However, after Davis left to become aide to General Philip Sheridan, Green assumed a prominent role at the monument.[65]

Some confusion has arisen over whether Casey or Green should receive the credit for designing and executing the pyramidion. The literature and records indicate that both men were equally responsible for the pyramidion. Casey may have assumed a greater role in creating the general plan of the roof by carefully observing the theories set down by Ambassador Marsh. Green said that "It was [under] Colonel Casey's own investigation and direction that the present outline of the pyramidion was adopted, giving to the monument that correctly proportioned crowning feature, without which, as in the original design, the shaft would have been architecturally little better than a chimney."[66]

On the other hand, there is every reason to believe that Green offered his engineering expertise on the detailed complexities of the design and the method of executing it. A detailed plan of the pyramidion is inscribed, "Designed and drawn under direction of Lt. Col. Thos. L. Casey, Corps of Engineers, by Bernard Richardson Green, Civil Engineer."[67] One writer has "ascribed the conception and working out of the plans for placing the pyramidion...on the shaft, plans adopted by the engineer in charge" to Green.[68]

In January 1884 Casey presented his newly developed ideas for the pyramidion to the Building Committee. His plan was unquestionably a radical change from the one originally proposed in 1878, but the Building Committee accepted it. Shortly afterwards the commission gave its approval.[69]

As the walls of the shaft neared completion, Casey's men began the preliminary task of assembling machinery and scaffolding to be used in constructing the roof. By the end of August 1884, the workers had fixed in place a derrick, mast, and boom to be used in setting the stone for the pyramidion. Men worked as long as 16 hours a day and until 9 p.m. under huge powerful lights that had been placed on nearby buildings.[70]

Work began on the roof in September. The delicate nature of the process of cutting the relatively thin marble slowed the cutters, forcing Casey to lay off some masons until enough dressed marble was on hand. In October, Casey increased the number of cutters to 93, which apparently solved the problem. Of the 262 pieces of marble needed to build the roof, the cutters had dressed all but 64 by the end of the month. This was enough to permit the masons to resume setting the stones. By the end of November, the last pieces of marble were cut and ready to be set.[71]

Although the new plan for the pyramidion made no reference to a metal apex, the capping of the roof with a metal apex was a significant achievement. The new plan had not included one, but Casey and Green tipped the apex with aluminum because its high conductivity would protect the monument from electrical storms. The metal apex was to serve as an integral part of a system of lightning rods. Casey and Green were also pleased because the pure aluminum would not tarnish when exposed to air and thus would not stain the marble.[72]

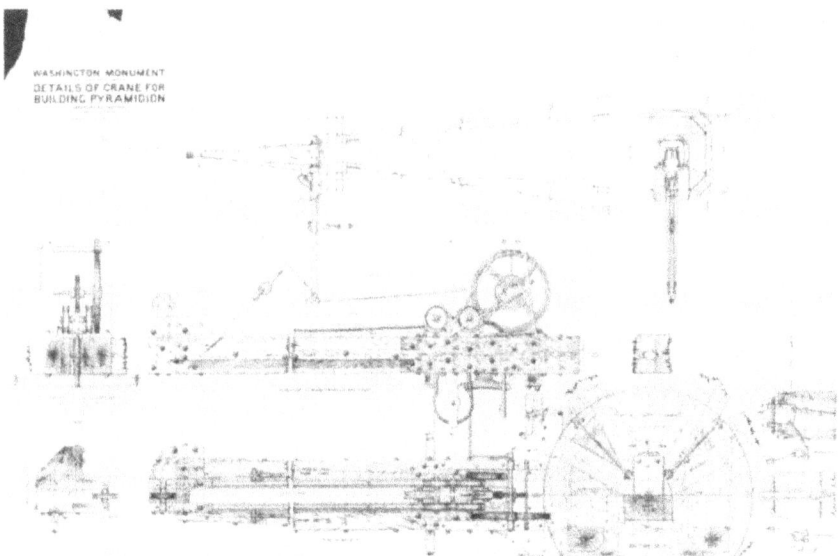

Structural diagrams for the crane that would set the stones for the pyramidion.
National Archives (Record Group 79, file 74.15-21).

To prepare this unusual piece of metal, Casey selected a retired Army colonel living in Philadelphia, William Frishmuth. To help Frishmuth make the tip, Casey sent him a wooden model that acted as a casting mould. When completed, the 100-ounce metal apex was 5.6 inches on each of its four sides measured at the base and 8.9 inches high. The apex had inscriptions on all four sides. On the north face was the inscription:

Joint Commission

at
Setting of Capstone.

Chester A. Arthur.
W.W. Corcoran, Chairman.
M.E. Bell.
Edward Clark.
John Newton.

Act of August 2, 1876.

The west face read:

Corner Stone Laid on Bed of Foundation
July 4, 1848.

First Stone at Height of 152 feet laid
August 7, 1880.

Capstone set December 6, 1884.

On the south side appeared:

Chief Engineer and Architect,
Thos. Lincoln Casey,
Colonel, Corps of Engineers.

Workmen finishing the capstone. *Library of Congress (photograph USZ62-24663).*

Assistants:
George W. Davis,
Captain, 14th Infantry.
Bernard R. Green,
Civil Engineer.
Master Mechanic,
P.H. McLaughlin.

The east side intoned:

Laus Deo.[73]

On the afternoon of December 6, surrounded by a group of dignitaries, Casey had the honor of setting the 3,300 pound capstone and securing the aluminum apex to the copper rod that passed through the capstone. As he set the capstone in place, cannons roared a salute and the national flag was unfurled at the top of the monument. Although rain marred the event, the invited guests huddled at the top, while the general public viewed the event from the base.[74]

Master mechanic and chief supervisor P. H. McLaughlin readies the aluminum apex for setting by Thomas L. Casey. From a sketch made during the dedication for Harper's Weekly by S. H. Nealy. *Library of Congress.*

Only one task remained before the roof was finished. The plan called for nine small openings. Eight were to be windows. The ninth opening located just beneath the apex would allow the masons to exit onto wooden platforms to complete their work on the exterior.

While the walls of the shaft were rising, they were nearly perpendicular. A large opening of the well in the center afforded access to the exterior. However, because the side of the pyramidion gradually converged until there was little or no opening, Casey and Green had to devise a series of scaffolds at different levels. The masons and other workers could then exit from the nine openings at the top onto the different scaffolds. Wood ladders connected the scaffolds. When the pyramidion was finished, the uppermost scaffold was removed first, and as the men descended, they removed the lower scaffolds, finally reentering the monument through the openings.[75]

The eight windows would be placed in pairs near the base of each face of the pyramidion for visitors. Following Marsh's advice Casey placed marble shutters on these openings so they would blend into the obelisk. To make the shutters functional, Casey encased the marble slabs in bronze frames. He made the frames, hung upon revolving cranes, of a "statuary bronze" that was resistant to corrosion and would not stain the marble. Each of the four pairs of frames was built so that one shutter could open to the right while the other could open to the left. Three pairs of openings were each three feet wide by 18 inches high, while the fourth pair was three feet wide by 24 inches high. Each shutter had a padlock and bolt made of bronze, so the windows could be locked. "When the windows are closed by these shutters," said Casey, "the pyramidion is much improved in appearance, and the interior of [the] shaft is protected from storm waters, which would otherwise flow into them from the roof and flood the upper platforms."[76]

The contractor delivered the bronze frames in late January 1885, but the shutters were not installed until March. The pyramidion was now complete.

The pyramidion was built of marble slabs no more than seven inches thick. Each slab rested upon the projections of 12 marble ribs that were laid vertically. Although these ribs, three on each side of the shaft, sprang from the 470-foot level, they eventually converged at the top of the pyramidion. The pyramidion weighed 300 tons. In addition to the ribs, it consisted of 262 slabs of marble measuring 3,764 cubic feet. The capstone cuneiform keystone measured 5.16 feet from its base to the top. Each side of the base was three feet long. The aluminum tip fitted snugly at the top.[77]

Dedication

Long before the workmen finished the pyramidion and the monument was ready to receive its first visitors, the Society began preparations for the long-awaited dedication. After Casey reported that the superstructure would probably be completed in early 1885, the Society requested that Congress authorize the dedication of the monument so that adequate preparations could be made well in advance. The Society based preparations on Casey's estimates of work yet to be done. His estimates were optimistic but reasonable. Only serious inclement weather and an inadequate supply of marble could cause any error in his calculations. The Joint Commission agreed with the Society's request and notified Congress.[78]

On 13 May 1884, by a joint resolution, Congress created a special commission of five senators, eight representatives, and three members of the Society, to arrange for the dedication. As plans for the occasion progressed, Casey proceeded with his own arrangements. He ordered workers to remove the huge quantity of materials and temporary facilities that had accumulated on the grounds. They removed the blacksmith shop, scaffolding carrying the railroad track into the monument, and the derricks. Other temporary buildings were later destroyed as construction on the superstructure gradually diminished.[79]

The dedication was held on 21 February 1885, the day before Washington's birthday. No amount of formality and jubilation was spared. Ben Perley Poore, a witness to the event, recalled that the day of dedication was clear and cold. Snow covered the ground around the base of the shaft. A

The dedication ceremony, 21 February 1885. *Library of Congress (photograph USZ62-19647).*

keen wind that blew down the Potomac "made it rather uncomfortable." All of official and private Washington seems to have attended:

> The regular troops and the citizen soldiery were massed in close columns around the base of the monument, the Freemasons occupied their allotted position, and in the pavilion which had been erected were the invited guests, the executive, legislative, and judicial officers; officers of the army, the navy, the marine corps, and the volunteers; the Diplomatic Corps, eminent divines, jurists, scientists, and journalists, and venerable citizens representing former generations, the Washington National Monument Society, and a few ladies who had braved the Arctic weather.

President Arthur concluded the ceremony by declaring the monument dedicated from that time forth "to the immortal name and memory of George Washington." That evening fireworks lit up the Mall.[80]

Senator Sherman, W.W. Corcoran, and Casey all spoke. In his address, Casey simply described the monument he had helped complete. He emphasized the strength of the foundation—his major achievement—and the beauty and resistance of the shaft.

Chester A. Arthur.
Library of Congress.

Chapter VI

THE MONUMENT IS COMPLETED

Although the opening of the monument had already been celebrated, much still had to be done before the public could visit. When Casey estimated that he needed an additional $250,000 to complete the monument, he noted that this would be enough for the pyramidion and a number of important projects. He still had to finish the stairway and pave the floor of the shaft. The interior walls of the old section of the shaft needed plastering and the elevator car and engine had to be converted for passengers. Finally, electric lights had to be furnished for the interior, and the boiler had to be removed to the edge of the monument lot.[1]

After Casey essentially finished the pyramidion in 1884, he turned to his list of unfinished projects, which included the placement of a growing number of memorial stones in the monument and the completion of an aesthetically-pleasing terrace around the base of the obelisk. Casey estimated the cost of completing all these projects at about $166,800, assuming that the terrace would need only simple earth-filling and grading. A more elaborate design, such as one with a marble wall surrounding the shaft, would raise the cost to $612,300.[2]

By the end of 1884, the four iron columns of the elevator shaft rose 517 feet, permitting the elevator to go nearly that high. In the meantime, the four outer columns that supported the stair landings reached the 500-foot platform.[3] Much more remained to be done before the stairway and elevator were considered complete. Temporary wooden covers had been placed over the iron stairs and platforms to protect them from the construction work. After most of the major construction was completed, workmen had to remove the wooden covers and replace them with iron or steel plates. The stairway also needed metal handrails. Concerned about the potential fire hazard, Casey was anxious to replace them as soon as possible.

The machinery that operated the elevator could carry a 10-ton load at 50 feet a minute. Casey proposed to retain the speed but convert the elevator platform into a passenger car. He planned to add seats and soft linings to the walls and generally embellish the interior and exterior of the car.

Casey wanted to move the boiler house and dynamo engines that operated the elevator to the western part of the monument grounds. Underground pipes would channel the steam that ran the engines and the resulting exhaust fumes to and from the engines and the elevator. Casey also proposed a new boiler house, stack, and 80-horsepower boiler.[40]

After passage of the 1885 appropriation, Casey let a contract for the ironwork to replace the wooden treads and platform covers and add the handrails. Difficulties at the mill in rolling the steel treads of the stairs halted alterations to the engine, boiler house, and the elevator car along with other work until later in the year. After overcoming this problem, the contractor made such excellent progress that by February 1886 workers installed all the platform covers and stair treads and more than half the handrails.[5] By April even the handrails were completed and the ungalvanized iron painted. This work permitted visitors to ascend the monument. By the end of September more than 10,000 had walked up to the 500-foot platform.

In July 1886 Otis Brothers received a contract for alteration of the elevator machinery and construction of a passenger car. By the end of the year, this work was finished and successfully tested. In the meantime, contracts were issued for placement of two steam boilers and the pipe connections between them and the engine house.[6]

In his 1882 plan for a terrace, Casey suggested eliminating the two doorways that had been built according to the Mills design during the early stages of construction. These were large Egyptian-styled doorways 15 feet high by six feet wide. A heavy pediment and an entablature with a carved winged ball and asp surmounted each door.

The doorways conformed to the original design of a massive pantheon surrounding the lower part of the obelisk. Since the pantheon had been abandoned, Casey favored removing the doorways because they detracted from the "character of an obelisk" and lessened the structure's unity. He recommended closing them and replacing them with an entrance through a gallery running beneath the terrace leading to the eastern staircase and passing underneath the east wall of the obelisk.

By the end of 1884, Casey still believed that the doorways should be eliminated by closing them off with ashler marble that matched the rest of the shaft. He also maintained that an unobtrusive entrance could be built beneath the terrace. "This closing of the doors," said Casey, "will present the structure to the eye and mind as an obelisk pure and simple, and will undoubtedly add to the dignity and impressiveness of the structure."[7]

Shortly after making this statement, Casey changed his mind. A careful study convinced him that if a subterraneous passage was built under the terrace, it would be necessary to cut away a substantial mass of concrete in the upper portion of the foundation. While conceding that this might not necessarily injure the foundation because the cut would be located at the cross section of the foundation where there was the least resistance, he recommended that the commission abandon the plan.

He proposed instead that they close the west doorway with a thin wall of marble that matched the shaft, and that they reduce the opening of the east doorway to eight feet, leaving it the only entrance to the monument. This doorway would be shut by two marble doors, the exterior surface of which would be flush with the face of the wall and uniformly lined up with the bond.[8]

The commission quickly approved Casey's revised plan. Casey contracted with Hugh Sisson for the marble pieces to enclose one doorway and shorten the second. Meanwhile, two stonecutters removed the architraves and lintels that jutted out from the doorways. The two marble doors revolved upon heavy bronze hinges. Each leaf weighed over one-half ton and was supported by a steel friction roller. The crew completed this work by the end of 1885.[9]

Casey had always worried about protecting the monument from damage by lightning. He thought it had been imprudent not to protect against lightning during construction. He supplied the unfinished structure with lightning rods and used the four Phoenix columns that supported the elevator shaft as electrical conductors. The cast iron shoes at the bottom of the columns were attached to the drum pit beneath the floor of the shaft. These shoes were then connected to .75-inch soft copper rods that led to the bottom of a well in the center of the foundation. After the copper rods were inserted in the well, it was filled with clean sharp sand to 15.67 feet. The four columns, lengthened during construction, continued to act as lightning conductors. During the five years it took to finish the shaft it was never damaged by electrical storms.

When the walls of the obelisk were enclosed at the pyramidion, four copper rods .75 inches in diameter were run from each of the four columns to the capstone. From there they were joined together with one 1.5-inch copper rod. While passing vertically through the capstone, this copper rod was screwed into the aluminum apex. This system of conductors was completed in January 1885.

The system soon had a test. In April lightning struck near the top, but caused no damage. The second storm in June damaged the capstone. Without delay, Casey consulted a team of experts who recommended that the interior conductors be connected by a system of rods and a greater number of points, all located upon the exterior of the pyramidion.[10]

Casey added four half-inch copper rods, "fastened by a band to the aluminum terminal and led down the corners to the base of the pyramidion." There the rods passed inward through the masonry and were jointed to the iron columns. The exterior rods, each more than 60 feet long, were also connected at two intermediate points to the iron columns by means of copper rods either .75 inches or .5 inches in diameter. In all, 16 rods connected the exterior system of conductors with the interior conducting columns. Where the exterior rods at the corners "cross the eleven highest horizontal joints of the masonry of the pyramidion, they are connected to each other all around by other copper rods sunk into those joints." Casey gold plated and tipped with aluminum all of the exterior rods, couplings, and fittings. They were studded every five feet with copper points three inches long. There were 200 of these points in all.[11]

The revised system of conductors that Casey had installed that year appeared to solve the problems. At the end of 1886 Casey reported that the new system had "fully answered all expectations." Even a heavy electrical storm on 22 May 1886 "failed to produce any disruptive effects." By 1900, there was no evidence that electrical storms had caused any damage to the monument.[12]

In January 1885 a contract was issued for an interior lighting system of 75 incandescent electric lamps, each with 16 candle power. The dynamo and cables of the system could produce enough power to light 125 lamps. From the floor of the monument to the 200-foot level two lights were fixed to each platform, and from this point to the 480-foot level there was only one to each platform. The dynamo, designed to produce 2,000 candle power, was set up in an enlarged engine house built south of the monument in 1886. The lighting system was installed by the end of 1885.[13]

Casey asked that a board of engineers review the lighting system. After studying the board's report, Casey developed some ideas to improve it. He proposed adding eight interior lamps, most of which would be placed as far up as the 517-foot level. Casey also recommended readjustment of wires and the electrical plant. This work was finished in January 1887. By 1894, 98 lamps lit the interior of the shaft. The four serving the passenger elevator contained 20 candle power. All the rest contained 16. Westinghouse produced the 25-horsepower engine that powered the dynamo.[14]

As the superstructure neared completion in 1884, Casey noticed that the backing of the first 150 feet of the interior walls consisted of roughly constructed rubble masonry. Many of the joints collected water from the condensation that ran down the face of the walls. The water absorbed into the walls destroyed the stone. Casey first suggested plastering this portion of the interior face with Portland cement mortar, rubbed down and lined off as coarse ashlar. Several months later, he reconsidered his proposal and suggested plastering only the lower portions of the shaft. Any imperfect joints above that area could also be repointed.[15] Neither plan was carried out, and nothing was done about the problem for many years.

In 1886 the floor of the monument was paved with blue stone flagging arranged in pleasing patterns. At that same time the drum pit and trench that held the main shaft of the engine were covered with wrought- and cast-iron plates.[16]

When Casey assumed charge of construction at the monument, he immediately measured and recorded the inscriptions on all the memorial stones fixed to the walls of the unfinished obelisk. Although it would be several years before additional stones could be fixed, Casey needed this information for his plans. In the meantime, he stored all the unfixed memorial stones in the lapidarium.[17]

The editors of *The American Architect and Building News* considered the memorial stones to be in "poor taste." The stones became objects of ridicule and misinformation. One source said that the Joint Commission would no longer use the memorial stones. This was not true. Although Casey showed some unwillingness to include all the memorial stones, he was satisfied that most of them would eventually be installed.[18]

By July 1878, the Society had received 189 memorial stones, and 92 had been fixed to the walls of the unfinished shaft. In removing the six feet of walls from the top, Casey had to remove eight of these stones, which he stored in the lapidarium along with the others. Casey wisely decided against fixing any more memorial stones until the walls of the superstructure were complete and the bond in the masonry had time to strengthen. He suggested cutting the stones to a three to six-inch thickness and fastening them into depressions in the walls. Bronze expansion bolts with ornamental nuts would secure the stones. Casey recommended that memorial stones accepted in the future measure no more than two feet by five feet and three to six inches thick. The Joint Commission approved the proposal.[19]

When the superstructure was completed, Casey began to arrange for the insertion of the memorial stones. He also planned to repair several stones already fixed to the walls that had deteriorated so much that their inscriptions could no longer be read. Casey proposed to the Building Committee that the 53 stones presented by states, foreign countries, cities, and societies should be put in the walls first. These were installed in June 1885 between the 160-foot and 230-foot platforms. Stonemasons reduced the thicker blocks before inserting them into depressions in the granite ashlar that varied from four to seven inches. Contrary to Casey's original plan, iron wedges, cement mortar, grouting, and pointing held the stones in place. Nine of the newly inserted stones were gifts from foreign countries, ten were from cities, nine were from Masonic temples, six from Odd-Fellow societies, four from the Sons of Temperance, and two from miscellaneous sources. The remaining 51 stones, which represented local groups, organizations, and individuals, were left to be inserted later.[20]

Throughout the next several years, masons installed memorial stones wherever space was available. This largely depended on congressional appropriations, which diminished substantially after the superstructure was completed. As a result, only a few stones could be installed each year, while additional ones kept arriving as gifts from various sources. By the end of 1888, 40 stones remained to be inserted. Eventually nearly all were installed; by 1929, the walls contained 187.[21]

The pantheon that Mills designed for the base of the monument excited considerable controversy long after the monument was completed.

Although Casey abandoned the Mills design, many still felt that some effort, no matter how simple or plain, should be made to enhance the beauty of the grounds. The artist Larkin G. Mead suggested to the Joint Commission that his bas-reliefs portraying the life of George Washington be used as part of an elaborate terrace at the base of the monument. Pressured by some members of Congress who liked the idea, the Joint Commission directed Casey in March 1882 to study the possibility of constructing a terrace that would contain a retaining wall, walks, and landscaping and use Mead's bronze bas-reliefs.[22]

As usual, Casey answered promptly. His plan incorporated a terrace supported by a masonry wall surmounted by a stone balustrade. Double staircases on all four sides of the monument would lead to the top of the terrace. On the blank walls of the terrace between the flights of these sets of steps, Mead would set his four bas-reliefs. Although the monument was an Egyptian obelisk "admitting no ornamentation," the terrace could be "capable of extensive and splendid ornamentation."

The steam engine for driving the elevator machinery within the shaft and the engine's boiler would be concealed within the terrace. The smoke flue could run underground to a vertical chimney.

Casey recommended closing the two doorways at the base of the obelisk and entering by a gallery under the top of the terrace, that would lead from the eastern staircase under the present east door. The doorways could be covered with thin marble walls, "the bond of the masonry to agree with that of the faces of the Monument."

Casey suggested that the Joint Commission ask three eminent sculptors and architects to propose a design for the terrace.[23] Those who advocated the Mills design or something similar were apparently vocal when Casey drew up his plan for the terrace. Was he influenced by their appeal? It would seem so. Although much less elaborate than the Mills design, Casey's plan for the terrace contained substantial ornamentation. When Casey prepared his plan, the question of the doorways to the shaft had not been settled, although he was later forced to alter this feature.[24]

The commission approved Casey's plan and forwarded it to the Joint Committee on Public Buildings and Grounds of Congress with the suggestion that it appoint a commission consisting of architects and artists to review the design. The plan did not fare well in Congress. Although several congressmen showed some sympathy for it, particularly those who objected to a plain base, no one was willing to reopen the debate that had surrounded the Mills design. More important, perhaps, no one in Congress was anxious to appropriate more money for the monument than was absolutely necessary. Although by 1884 Casey's plan was still being considered, it was clear to many that it would probably never be executed.

Casey next offered a less elaborate proposal. He wanted to fill in the earth around the existing terrace and extend this filling far enough from the monument that it would gradually fade into surrounding areas, giving the mound a more natural landscape. He suggested planting trees and shrubs and constructing concrete or stone approaches around the mound. Casey estimated that this plan would require 275,000 cubic yards of earth. The design would cost $166,800, much less than the $612,300 needed for his first plan. Correctly sensing the mood in Congress, the Joint Commission supported the second plan.[25]

While Congress and the committee debated the question of the terrace, a related problem arose. In December 1884, during construction of the obelisk, Casey observed that when added weight caused the shaft to move, the two north corners of the structure settled first. He believed that the northside pond, called Babcock Lake, caused the earth to settle. This pond, the remnant of an old canal basin, was used for breeding carp and for ice skating in winter. Much of its bed consisted of soft mud and organic deposits. The surface of the pond was level with the bottom of the monument's foundation, and the bottom of the pond at its deepest point was about four feet beneath the bottom of the foundation. Only 250 feet separated the edge of the pond and the foundation.

Casey observed that when the pond's waters were drawn away, springs appeared along the south shore that deposited fine sand on the shore. He theorized that these spring waters came from a subterranean body of water south of the pond that carried sand originating in the thin strata underlying and surrounding the monument's foundation. If it continued, warned Casey, this action "might possibly degrade the bed of the foundation...and endanger its stability." To minimize this possibility and at the same time improve the terrace's landscape, Casey recommended that they fill in Babcock Lake to its banks. He estimated that he would need 83,000 cubic yards of earth.[26]

Casey's argument appeared valid, but Congress was unwilling to eliminate a pond that had been used by the community for so many years. To appease Congress, Casey suggested a trench in the bed of the pond along the south bank deep enough to cut off the sand strata.[27] The Joint Commission preferred Casey's original proposal. The commission stood firm, and Congress finally conceded. The monument's stability was important enough to receive proper congressional attention.

In March 1887 a contract was awarded for filling in earth at the base of the monument as well as Babcock Lake. Three months later another contract was issued for a 10-foot-wide pavement around the base of the shaft, which was completed in November. Congress had to pass special legislation to permit large quantities of earth to pass through the city.[28] So much earth was needed for the new terrace and pond that "literally a hill" was removed from one site in southwest Washington. The slope of the grounds was now "an inviting stretch of park land, the venue [sic] of innumerable public gatherings."[29] By 1887, the terrace sloped "in all directions to meet the natural surface at distances of 350 to 450 feet from the shaft."[30]

In late 1886 Casey recommended to the Building Committee that the monument be opened to the public. He proposed that the monument be placed in the hands of a permanent government agency that would operate and maintain the structure and enforce rules whenever necessary. Only the year before he had warned the commission of vandalism by "thoughtless visitors." When the commission recommended that the War Department maintain the monument because it would take congressional action, the commission directed Casey to prepare a letter to Congress.[31]

Supported by Casey's letter, in January 1887 the commission formally requested Congress to place the monument under the management of the War Department. The commission suggested that the War Department "preserve [the monument] from injury and defacement,...supervise the operation of the machinery connected therewith, and assist in its inspection by visitors; and that a suitable sum should be annually appropriated for...maintenance...."[32]

"In the Elevator," an 1887 etching from *A Souvenir of the Federal Capital*, by Hutchins and Moore.
Library of Congress
(photograph USZ62-59907).

Congress failed to respond quickly, perhaps feeling that the monument was not finished enough to accept visitors on a large scale. More likely, Congress was reluctant to pass an appropriation sufficient to operate the monument. Congress' failure to pass an appropriation compelled the commission to shut down the elevator service. Casey dismantled the steam engine, electric dynamo, and boiler to preserve them.

This did not stop the curious, averaging 125 a day, who came from all parts of the country to climb the monument stairs. Withing one year about 27,000 people had visited the monument. Despite a guard posted at the bottom and another at the top, vandalism became a serious problem.

Finally, the Joint Commission instructed Casey to close the monument indefinitely to all visitors.[33]

Work on the monument had come so far by 1888 that Casey's guiding hand was no longer necessary. On April 2, he was relieved of duty as Engineer in Charge of Construction of the Washington National Monument. Two days later Colonel John M. Wilson of the Corps of Engineers assumed the job. By then, there was little more to do on the monument than complete the terrace and construct a marble administration building on the grounds. The cost of building the monument stood at $1,187,710, one-fourth of which had been raised by the Society for the first phase of construction.[34]

After finishing his work at the monument, Casey served as president of the Board of Fortifications and Public Works in New York City and as a member of the Lighthouse Board. Promoted to brigadier general in July 1888, Casey was then appointed Chief of the Corps of Engineers. Although he retired in 1895, he supervised the completion of the Library of Congress, until his death in 1896.

After Casey's departure, the commission continued to pressure Congress for War Department control over the operation of the monument. By law the department already controled the monument grounds. Noting how far the construction had advanced, the commission recommended that it be abolished and that the Society continue to operate in an advisory capacity to the War Department. Finally, it suggested that Congress appropriate enough money to pay the wages of a permanent staff at the monument consisting of one custodian, one steam engineer, one assistant steam engineer, one fireman, one assistant fireman, one car conductor, one floor attendant, one attendant at the top, and three day and night watchmen. The commission estimated it would cost $10,500 annually to operate the monument.

Almost two years had passed since the Joint Commission had made its first request to Congress. On 2 October 1888, Congress finally passed legislation incorporating most of the recommendations made by the commission. Congress dissolved the Joint Commission and appointed the War Department custodian of the monument. The Corps of Engineers ultimately gained responsibility for the monument, which was assigned to the Officer in Charge of Public Buildings and Grounds.[35]

The monument, now officially opened to the general public, immediately became the object of both praise and scorn. The furor that began over the monument's design long before it was constructed continued well into the 20th century. While laymen marveled at this almost superhuman effort, serious and professional observers actively criticized the monument. Some reflected the views of earlier critics who had rejected the Mills design in toto and who were opposed to any of the modifications suggested by Casey.

Those who despised the monument regarded it as the abomination of the ages. In 1884 one critic noting Casey's work in strengthening the foundation facetiously added that "it is...to be regretted that ages are likely to elapse before the monument will fall down."[36] Strongly condemning the fact that the Mills peristyle was not incorporated in the monument's base, the same writer contended that:

> There is some satisfaction in reflecting that the United States now possesses the tallest building in the new world, but this cheap glory will not last long, and when it is gone there will be little else about the monument to be proud of. It is curious to see how completely the original design of the monument has been forgotten. As a part of Mills's novel and thoroughly classical conception, the obelisk, rising from the stupendous colonnade which supported it, was well-proportioned and elegant, but without that support it is an ugly chimney, and nothing more; and the ridiculous attempts which have been made ever since Mills's design was abandoned to argue people into the idea that the monument, as it now stands, is beautiful, or symbolic, or Egyptian, or anything else but a lanky pile of stone, simply illustrate the dullness and hypocrisy which rein supreme among us in regard to artistic matters. If it were not for the enormous cost of carrying out the original plan, with its peristyle of marble columns a hundred feet high, we should be strongly in favor of returning to it....[37]

Although critics of the monument had not been enamored of the classical pantheon, they were convinced that as it stood, the monument was incomplete. Even a simple base, these critics agreed, was better than none.[38]

Others gradually became convinced, though hesitatingly, that the obelisk did possess some fine qualities. As one early critic pointed out, "Those who wish to find beauty in it...will say that it befits republican simplicity and the rugged honesty and virtue of Washington."[39] There were those, however, who, while accepting the monument as a *fait accompli,* would continue to argue that the base or terrace was less than satisfactory.

Many people accepted and praised Casey's final design. Some favorably compared the monument and the man it sought to memorialize. One writer declared that the monument typified the character of George Washington, "lofty in its grandeur, plain in its simplicity, and white in its purity."[40] Perhaps the most lauditory opinion was contained in a 1902 report by Frederick Law Olmsted, Jr., and Charles Moore:

> Taken by itself, the Washington Monument stands not only as one of the most stupendous works of man, but also as one of the most beautiful of human creations. Indeed, it is at once so great and so simple that it seems to be almost a work of nature. Dominating the entire District of Columbia, it has taken its place with the Capitol and the White House as one of the three foremost national structures.[41]

Others viewed the monument as an object of "magnificent simplicity."[42]

Chapter VII

THE LATER YEARS

The Washington Monument was declared officially opened on 9 October 1888, with the passage of an appropriation by Congress of just over $10,000. In succeeding years this figure grew until it reached around $16,000 or $17,000. These appropriations did not include the cost of replacing expensive equipment or extensive maintenance, both of which demanded special legislation.[1]

Seven days after the law was passed, the boilers, engines, electric dynamos, and elevator were in working condition. Colonel John M. Wilson, the Officer in Charge of Public Buildings and Grounds, had overall responsibility of the monument, but George M. Thomas, a civilian who bore the title alternately of Custodian, Clerk, and Superintendent, ran the daily operations. His salary was $125 a month.[2] In the 1920s the Office of Public Buildings and Grounds was reorganized under the new title of Director of Public Buildings and Public Parks of the National Capital.

The Sundry Civil Act passed by Congress on 2 October 1888, provided for the staff of 11 that Casey had recommended the previous year. The custodian and three watchmen had already been working for Casey for several months. Colonel Wilson filled the remaining seven positions. So many candidates applied for these few jobs that he complained that in his "long life, I have seldom had such a rush for a few places and I have tried my best to satisfactorily fill them. ...The demands upon me are simply overwhelming and my regret is that it is not in my power to give employment to the hundreds that are constantly seeking it."[3] Wilson observed that those he selected, particularly firemen, steam engineers, and elevator operators "must be experts" in their field, able to handle any type of emergency. He promoted two former laborers at the monument to floor attendants.[4] Over the years the number of employees varied slightly, depending frequently upon appropriations. The number ranged between 6 and 12, but usually remained at 11.

Congress fixed eight hours as the maximum workday. Wilson noted that if the hours of operation were extended, the monument would need to hire four additional employees: an assistant engineer, an assistant fireman, an attendant, and a car conductor. This would mean a $1,000 increase in operating costs.[5] There is little evidence that the staff was ever increased much beyond the original 11, even after the hours were extended to include Sundays and legal holidays.

In 1902 the staff, with the exception of the firemen, were required to wear uniforms comparable to those of employees at the Capitol and the Corcoran Art Gallery. The employees paid for their uniforms, which consisted of blouses and caps.[6]

The Tidal Basin, c. 1910, with the monument in the background. *Library of Congress.*

Visitors

The monument had generated widespread interest even while it was being built. Before it was completed, and long before the elevator worked, thousands of visitors ascended the stairs and marveled at this unique structure. Although Casey and his assistants regulated these early visitors by issuing passes, 10,041 people visited the monument between April (when this policy was instituted) and September 1886.The staff faithfully kept the logbooks. They recorded the daily attendance of visitors and the number that either used the elevator or climbed the 893 steps to the top. During the next eight months the number grew to 27,000. The absence of an elevator apparently was no obstacle to the curious.[7]

After the monument officially opened in October 1888, attendance soared. In the first nine months 613,175 people visited the monument. By the turn of the century, 1,696,718 came, and by mid-1914, some 4,095,088 visitors were counted.[8]

During its first years of operation, the monument maintained restricted hours, Monday through Friday, nine to five. Pressured by several private groups, in 1914 Congress approved a Sundry Civil Act containing a provision for an additional appropriation to keep the monument open on Sundays and legal holidays. The new policy was inaugurated on August 1. On weekdays the monument was open from 9:00 A.M. to 4:30 P.M., and on Sundays and holidays it was open from 12:30 P.M. to 4:40 P.M. The number of visitors also increased. During the fiscal year ending June 1915, 30,610 people visited the monument on 48 Sundays and seven holidays.[8]

By February 1923 a grand total of 6,156,302 people had visited the monument; of this number, 4,561,249 used the elevator and 1,595,053 hardy visitors ascended the stairs. By June 1931 the monument's staff had registered 10,048,776 visitors to the monument since its opening, 7,319,347 of whom used the elevator while the other 2,729,429 climbed the stairs.[10]

Extenuating circumstances sometimes closed the monument. When Presidents Harding and Wilson died, the monument was closed out of respect. When a coal strike gripped the nation and there was little fuel to operate the monument, visitors were also turned away.

Although individuals comprised the bulk of visitors, special large groups such as societies and associations were also welcomed. When the Grand Army of the Republic encamped in Washington for six days in September 1892, more than 30,000 members visited the top of the monument and another 20,000 entered the monument without ascending. In August 1895 Congress permitted the Knights of Pythias to occupy the grounds around the monument. In what must have been an unusual event, on the evenings of 12 and 14 May 1899, the monument, with its elevator and electric lights operating, played host to the American Society of Mechanical Engineers, which held its annual meeting in Washington.[11]

Requests for permission to use the monument for personal gain or for some unusual purpose frequently beseiged the custodian. In this respect, the monument was no different from other great attractions, such as the contemporaneous Statue of Liberty in New York Harbor. The custodian rejected demands that he considered undignified and unsafe. One couple sought permission to be married "at an elevated position" in the monument with a bridal party of five or six. A congressman even requested that one of his constituents be granted permission to scatter his wife's ashes from the window of the monument.[12]

Other requests were more consonant with the dignity of the monument. The Liberty Loan Committee of the Treasury Department received permission to suspend a large sign on the north side of the monument just below the windows to further the sale of Victory Notes. A powerful searchlight on the nearby Arlington building illuminated the sign at night.[13] Another individual was granted permission to study the characteristics of atmospheric currents from the top of the monument by releasing a small balloon attached to a fine thread from the window.[14]

In the annual report for fiscal year 1897, Colonel Theodore A. Bingham, who had replaced Wilson as Officer in Charge of Public Buildings and Grounds, boasted that "it is a noteworthy fact that no one has yet been killed or fatally injured either during the erection of the Monument or its administration since completion."[15] After he issued that statement, however, one worker plunged to his death while painting the interior iron. In 1924 a woman attempting to save her three-year-old-child who had slipped on the stairs, fell through the guard rail from the 400-foot level and was killed. The child was found, cut and bruised but otherwise safe, on the stairs.[16]

In 1915 there was a suicide when a woman leaped to her death from the 480-foot landing. In the 1920s two people jumped from the windows of the pyramidion.[17] These deaths led to the construction of a third guard rail on the stairway and iron bars on the windows.

The Office of Public Buildings and Grounds worked to improve the visitors' comfort. To enhance the lighting system, the number of lights was increased and the dynamo and wiring were rebuilt. Additional lights were placed wherever visitors congregated to wait for the elevator. In 1923 new cables and conduits were installed, adding to the power, light, and heat. The local power and light company did the work and controlled the power, obviating the services of one engineer and two firemen.[18]

In 1904 a small reception room was built on the ground floor. The frame of the room was made of steel I beams and channel irons and the walls and ceiling of concrete. The floor was composed of mosaic and marble wainscot. The room was lighted with electric bulbs, heated by steam, and furnished with four oak settees.[19] This room contributed significantly to the comfort of visitors, who often had a long wait for the elevator.

In 1890 steam pipes were installed around the walls of the lower floor, providing heat to visitors waiting for the elevator. The heat from these pipes could be felt as high as the 250-foot level. That same year a storm door was installed at the entrance to the monument. This was replaced later by a revolving door.[20]

Over the years various safety features were added. In 1927 a third guard rail was added to the stairway and a metal grill covering the three guard rails was installed to prevent accidents of the kind that had occurred in 1924.[21]

In 1931 red lights were installed on one of the windows on each side of the pyramidion to warn aircraft. Experiments were also conducted using different types of floodlights and searchlights to light up the monument as a further warning to approaching aircraft. As a result, it was possible to prepare specifications designed to eventually illuminate the exterior.[22]

Vandalism and other public nuisances had been a growing problem ever since visitors were permitted to walk up the monument in 1886. Souvenir hunters chipped away at the memorial stones and drew graffiti on the walls. Seedy characters hawking their wares frequented the grounds. Casey and his assistants, seeing the damage, appealed as early as December 1885 to the Joint Commission to curb these practices. Casey warned at one point, "It would seem proper that some action should be taken to prevent these occurrences, which if continued may impair the stability of certain parts of the structure."[23]

The commission instructed Casey to establish a code of conduct and police regulations to govern behavior at the monument. Whatever Casey drafted would have to be transmitted to Congress, which legislated regulations. Casey immediately drew up a set of rules, and in early January 1886 Chairman Corcoran submitted them to the Senate Committee on Public Buildings and Grounds. The rules tried to cover the violations that had been committed at the monument up to that point. They restricted walking around the monument to roads and paths. They forbade the sale or advertisement of any article and the solicitation of any kind of contributions on monument grounds. The regulations prohibited several mischievous acts, but most importantly forbade the marking, defacing, and disfiguring of any part of the monument "or to chip off fragments or pieces from any of the stone, iron, or other parts of the completed structure or its surroundings. ...." Violations of regulations would be punished by a fine of at least $5, imprisonment for 15 days or more, or both. For serious offenses in which damage exceeded $100, the offender would be remanded for trial and if found guilty imprisoned for six months to five years. The proposed regulations gave monument employees the right to assist the police in arresting offenders.[24]

Congress took more than one year to pass the required legislation, much to the frustration of the commission, which was anxious to be "clothed with the much needed authority to fully protect the monument from any distinctive act of vandalism." In the meantime, vandalism continued unabated, as visitors defaced and mutilated many parts of the structure with impunity.[25]

By the end of 1888, the rules and regulations laid down by Congress had been superseded by a code of conduct prepared by the Office of Public Buildings and Grounds. These rules were designed for the monument's employees as well as for the visitor. In addition to outlining the responsibilities of each employee, they established hours of visitation and the number of times that the elevator would be operated in one day. They gave the watchman the power to arrest any person committing malicious mischief and required all employees to notify the watchman of any violation that would lead to arrest.

Whenever a new officer was appointed to head the Office of Public Buildings and Grounds, it was customary for him to establish his own rules on running the monument.[26] Serious violations leading to the defacement of government property were governed by the United States Statutes, which provided "a penalty of not more than fifty dollars for each and every offense." An offender unable to pay the fine would serve six months in a workhouse.[27] The Officer in Charge of Public Buildings and Grounds insisted that his watchmen use their powers of arrest, anyone not doing so would be fired. Watchmen were not "figure heads," said Colonel Wilson.[28]

The regulations did not deter persistent violators because there were too few employees to enforce them. Between July 1888 and June 1889 the Officer in Charge of Public Buildings and Grounds reported numerous instances of vandalism, particularly grafitti and the defacement of memorial tablets. In 1904, 30 cast iron signs warning visitors against committing any acts of vandalism were placed on alternate landings. One of the most flagrant violators removed three of the four silver letters from the stone presented by the State of Nevada.[29]

Vandalism continued unabated over the years, much of it against the memorial stones. Some youths threw stones and other objects from the windows of the pyramidion. They were arrested and brought to justice, but most often the offenders went unpunished.

The Memorial Stones and the Bronze Plaque

Memorial stones continued to arrive long after the monument was completed. Many of them were reduced and inserted in walls wherever there was space. Placements continued through the 1920s. Many stones that were already hanging and had been vandalized or that showed signs of wear were repaired and cleaned periodically.

During the final years of construction, a serious question arose that plagued the custodians long afterwards. In 1887 the Society had offered to hang a bronze plaque on the ground floor. No one would have objected had it not contained the names of several illustrious members of the Society without adequately mentioning the many government officials and agencies, including the Corps of Engineers, who had contributed so much to the monument's construction. Without intending to embarrass the Society, the Joint Commission, probably at Casey's insistence, rejected the plaque on the grounds that it contained too much detail. The commission had no objection to a plaque being hung in the Marble Lodge that was to be built as an administration building, provided that the inscription was shortened to contain only the names of those who were directly identified with the monument's history and construction.

The matter was dropped until 1890, when the Society again proposed to place a bronze plaque on the south wall of the first floor. The tablet, which weighed about 900 pounds, was in the final stages of completion and was probably the same one offered to the Joint Commission three years earlier. When Colonel Wilson forwarded the request to General Casey, who was then the Chief of Engineers, Casey advised the Secretary of War that:

> The inscription in bronze... goes too far in some directions and not far enough in others, and as a history of construction of the obelisk is misleading and unjust. Work done by the general government in completing the monument as it stands today, having first purchased from the society the unfinished and faulty designed structure, is scarcely alluded to, and the presentation of the matter is not one that should be handed down to posterity. The inscription is largely an aggregation of names and persons to be perpetuated in the monument to George Washington, many of whom had nothing to do with the construction of the obelisk, while hundreds who subscribed their money and were members of the society, are not recorded. A similar inscription was brought to the attention of the Joint Commission during the last administration, and its introduction in the monument was not authorized.

With Casey's words to support him, Secretary of War Redfield Proctor rejected the Society's request. There the matter stood for several years.[32] The finished tablet was stored in the Marble Lodge where the Society had an office. After Casey's death, the Society tried anew to have the plaque hung in the monument, but this also failed.[33] Although no more was heard on the subject after this attempt, the precedent had been set for accepting similar plaques. Requests by various groups in later years to hang such tablets were rejected "not only for reasons of taste, but also for reasons of policy.[34]

Structural Problems

In 1884 and 1885 Casey recommended a process that would seal the interior joints of the monument's walls and halt the slow deterioration of the stone caused by the high levels of condensation.[35] The Joint Commission did nothing, and the problem plagued the custodians later. The condensation was so intense at times that attendants wore overshoes and raincoats to keep dry. By the turn of the century, the interior condensation began penetrating the joints of the outer walls, causing the marble ashler to discolor and disintegrate at the joints.

Although no longer officially associated with the monument, Bernard Green remained interested in its development. He observed that because the stone in the lower portion of the shaft had been joined together with poor mortar and rubble, the heavy condensation that inevitably formed penetrated the joints of the stone, causing the lime mass to disintegrate and to form "scales or barnacles" on the white marble. Other professional observers pessimistically wondered how long this condition could last without shortening the life of the monument. One geologist and head curator of the National Museum believed that if the condition continued, the chemical action would eventually destroy the structure. He believed that the only way to cure this deterioration, which he referred to as a "tuberculous" condition, was to shore the lower 190 feet of wall, remove the outer facing, and replace it with granite.[36]

This extreme remedy was based on a prevailing concept that favored the use of granite over marble. Others offered more moderate solutions. The Obelisk Water Proofing Company suggested its Carfall process of rehabilitation. The company was convinced that the condensation formed in the interior was not only seepage penetrating the walls, but that heavy precipitation was also causing the marble to deteriorate. If the exterior walls of the obelisk were waterproofed by a chemical used by their firm, they argued, the monument would then be covered by a "sheet of tin," preventing any water from damaging the surface. The Office of Public Buildings and Grounds denied that precipitation caused major damage and declared that waterproofing the exterior was futile.[37]

Disagreements over the cause of the disintegration and what could be done to prevent it continued for many years. In the meantime, nothing was done. In 1931 the Director of Public Buildings and Public Parks of the National Capital declared that the monument was deteriorating so rapidly "that definite action for its preservation will soon have to be taken." The exterior marble was spalling badly, and he feared that falling stone fragments would injure someone. He reported that if Casey's recommendations had been heeded, the problem could have been avoided or at least minimized. The director announced that, "studies and estimates for the necessary remedial steps" had begun.[38] While it now seemed that some action would finally be taken, the ultimate responsibility would soon be out of the hands of the Corps of Engineers. In 1933, the National Park Service assumed control of the monument.

The elevator continually vexed the Office of Public Buildings and Grounds. The same elevator and machinery that were used in constructing the obelisk served visitors many years after the monument opened officially. The machinery was run by steam generated in boilers connected to an engine by pipes laid in trenches cut beneath the surface. The steam caused considerable corrosion within the boilers and pipes, which then had to be dismantled and cleaned. Moreover, because the machine operated continually, the cables that hoisted the elevator car became so worn that they often had to be replaced, shutting down the elevator for several days. The expense of maintaining the elevator proved extremely high.

The monument's steam-driven elevator engine. *Library of Congress (photograph USZ62-15295).*

Technicians of Otis Brothers and later inspectors of the District of Columbia checked the elevators monthly for serious defects. The monument's staff also examined it each morning. Colonel Wilson insisted that every precaution be taken to see that there were no malfunctions. He cautioned his custodian that "the moment you have reasonable grounds for belief that the elevator...is not perfectly safe, you are hereby directed to suspend using it at once and to take...the necessary steps for immediate repairs."[39]

In spite of these precautions, many people remained concerned about the elevator's safety. Wilson moved quickly to allay these fears whenever he could. In one of his reports to the Chief of Engineers he stated, "It is believed that the elevator is as safe as it is possible for man to make it, and every effort is made to prevent accident; should an accident ever occur it will result from something which it was impossible to foresee."[40]

Despite these frequent assurances of safety, complaints continued. Some of them originated with the Society, which, as adviser to the War Department, felt obliged to call attention to the inadequacy of the elevator. The Society recognized that although the elevator may have represented the most advanced ideas available when it was installed, it had long since become obsolete and was poorly adapted to serve the increasing number of visitors. The Society suggested converting the elevator to electricity. The new elevator would move faster and hold more passengers.[41]

The elevator took about 10 to 12 minutes to ascend and descend the 500 feet. This discouraged many visitors from going up. Although the elevator was slow and frequently needed repairs, the stalwart visitor was not deterred. Bent on viewing the monument at any cost, he climbed to the top, unless the structure was shut down completely. The electrical system also had to be repaired often. When there was no electricity, kerosene lanterns were placed on each of the landings and visitors again walked to the top.

Colonel Bingham agreed that converting the system to electricity would be a decided improvement. He hoped that this conversion would come about some day, but he cautioned that installation and operating costs would be high. His observation reflected the parsimonious attitude of a Congress that had always kept its appropriations for the monument at as low a level as possible. Although he was certain that the existing elevator was safe, he nevertheless cryptically said: "The elevator service of this monument is a much more serious matter than is commonly understood, and while I am quite desirous...that everything connected with it should be of the very best, it is also true that careful consideration must be exercised in making any changes."[42]

The Society's suggestion finally produced some results. The problems surrounding the elevator became so serious that the Office of Public Buildings and Grounds pressed more aggressively for a new one. A more sympathetic Congress now listened carefully. In his report to the Chief of Engineers, Bingham said:

> Steam is carried 800 feet under ground with many pipe joints requiring continual care of their packing; one of the two boilers practically does nothing but keep this pipe hot. The elevator cage is 1,000 pounds heavier than need be; and so on.
>
> It would be very easy to substitute electric power. A small addition to the boiler house could be built to hold the dynamos; the current would be carried under ground where the steam pipes now are. A lighter elevator cage could be used, with a counterweight, so as to make the load on the dynamos as light as possible. The lighting of the Monument would not then require a separate dynamo.
>
> More than this, there would then be an independent source of power for lighting the grounds about the Monument and south of the Executive Mansion, and even for the use of the Executive Mansion itself and its front grounds.

He estimated the total cost of installing the electric system at $26,500.[43]

The arguments in favor of an electric elevator system were convincing, and in 1900 Congress passed the necessary appropriation. The new system, in operation the following year, was a decided improvement. The new elevator took five minutes in either direction. The car held as many as 35 passengers, the equivalent of a 10,920-pound load. It weighed 5,670 pounds, and its counterweight was 8,040 pounds. The dynamo produced 50 kilowatts and 250 volts.[44]

The new system required much less maintenance. Cables had to be changed because of the extensive use of the elevator; new cables installed in 1905 cost $2,500. They were each 1,070 feet long and 1-1/2 inches in diameter and consisted of six strands of the best steel wound around a hemp center. Tests showed that these cables had a tensile strength of 130,000 pounds.[45]

A casualty insurance company and local government agencies periodically inspected the elevator. The increased number of visitors created so much stress on the system that frequent inspections were extremely important for safety and efficiency.

Such heavy use soon made the equipment obsolete. In 1925, following a routine inspection, the Office of Public Buildings and Grounds estimated it would cost $10,000 to accomplish needed substantial repairs to the system. While the system was basically sound, it was old and mechanically obsolete. The Officer in Charge wisely recommended that instead of spending a large sum on repairs, they install a new and modern electric elevator. The War Department agreed and immediately submitted a request for an appropriation to Congress, which appropriated $30,000 "for extraordinary repairs and replacement of the elevator and machinery." The new equipment was completely installed in June 1926.[46]

The Marble Lodge

When Casey submitted his annual report to the commission in December 1886, he reported that only the terrace, or earth-filling, needed to be finished and a building for a watchman and for the public comfort had to be built. This small building, called the Marble Lodge, was the brainchild of the Society. It would serve as offices for the custodian and the Society, an archives for the monument's construction and Society's records, and a comfort station for visitors. The Society offered the commission $12,000 that it had raised and earned through investments to cover the cost of construction. Moreover, it wanted Casey to select the design and supervise the work.[47]

Once it was determined that the Marble Lodge was within the Joint Commission's responsibilities, Casey was immediately assigned to construct

Architect's rendering of the marble lodge. *National Archives (Record Group 79, file 74.20-3).*

the building. In May 1887 he asked the Washington architectural firm of William M. Poindexter and Company to prepare drawings. By September plans and specifications were in his hands.

Casey was to select a site that was neither so close that it detracted from the monument's appearance nor so distant that it inconvenienced visitors. At first Casey picked a spot 325 feet from the monument. The commission preferred a closer location, so he reluctantly selected one only 40 feet from the monument.

In the meantime, Wilson succeeded Casey and gave the contractor instructions to begin work on this site in April 1888. The Building Committee had second thoughts and switched to a site 480 feet east of the monument.[48]

Because the contractor had already begun work at the earlier site, some time was lost in making the change. Work on the new location started at the end of May 1888. Despite Wilson's persistent prodding the work progressed slowly at first. It soon became evident that the contractor would be unable to meet the September deadline specified in the contract. The Marble Lodge was finally finished in January 1889. Although the building cost the Society $10,720, it spent an additional $930 because of the change in location. The completed lodge was transferred to the United States under the custodianship of the Office of Public Buildings and Grounds.[49]

The Terrace and the McMillan Plan

The monument grounds continued to cause debate. In March 1887 a contract to fill in the earth around the monument and Babcock Lake was awarded. The contract was completed in December 1888, although at least twice Colonel Wilson complained to the contractor that he was using ashes, mortar, bricks, and other refuse contrary to the contract's provisions. Grading the grounds, beautifying the landscape, and building concrete and stone walks continued for several years. Drainpipes were also laid to improve drainage, a constant problem. Several thousand cubic yards of earth were bought for the grading, but several thousand more were received without cost to the government when various Washington contractors found the monument grounds a convenient place to dump their soil. Another 1,630 cubic yards of broken stone and concrete hauled to the monument as refuse by contractors, without cost to the government, were used for foundations to build walks and roadways surrounding the grounds. These new roadways and walks permitted the visitor to approach the monument from different directions.[50]

The monument grounds, an extensive park covering about 78 acres, became one of the most popular Washington attractions. In 1893 the Officer in Charge of Public Buildings and Grounds believed that this park was destined to become the Mecca for visitors from all over the country. The rapidly growing number of visitors in the years after its completion proved the enormous popularity of this park. Every effort, therefore, was made to keep the grounds looking as attractive as possible. Lawns were cut frequently, the landscape was properly maintained, paths and roads were repaired, gutters and drain traps were kept clean and in good working condition, and washouts were frequently repaired in and around the monument.[51]

The grounds became so popular that Congress, the Executive, and City Fathers constantly watched them. Preservation and beautification plans for the District of Columbia, particularly for the Mall, soon included the monument grounds. Although the idea of elaborate terraces, such as the one proposed by Mills' design, had not been entirely abandoned, it had lost favor in many artistic circles. Several plans were offered in and out of Congress to enhance the monument grounds as part of a broader plan to beautify the city of Washington, including the Mall and parks.

One far-reaching concept was the McMillan plan of 1901, named after Senator James McMillan of Michigan, sponsor of the bill. Although Senator McMillan spearheaded the plan, a commission consisting of such prominent building and landscape architects as Daniel H. Burnham, Charles F. McKim, Frederick Law Olmsted, Jr., and Augustus St. Gaudens, was responsible for the concept. The plan incorporated three major concepts—enhancing and enlarging the Mall, restoring L'Enfant's central theme of seeming to place the Washington Monument at the axes of the Capitol and the White House, and constructing a memorial to Abraham Lincoln at the north end of the Mall. The plan also included improvements for other parts of the District of Columbia.

The monument grounds were essential to the success of the McMillan plan. Echoing some of the arguments of the past, the commission said:

> At present the immediate surroundings of the Monument are so inadequate as to cause the beholder near at hand to lose that very sense of grandeur which it inspires when seen from a distance; and the lack of harmonious relationship between it and the great structures with which it comes into juxtaposition disturbs one's sense of fitness. No portion of the task set before the Commission has required more study and extended consideration than has the solution of the problem of devising an appropriate setting for the Monument; and the treatment here proposed is the one which seems best adapted to enhance the value of the Monument itself.

This same commission had praised the monument as being one of the "most stupendous works of man" and "one of the most beautiful of human creations."[52]

The commission favored an elaborate formal treatment. On the east side, a broad terrace would provide a base for the obelisk. On the west side, a long reflecting pool would extend to the proposed Lincoln Memorial. Finally, in the most controversial part of the plan, the commission proposed a huge stairway down to a sunken garden centered on a pool and fountain marking the intersection of the White House and Capitol axes.[53]

The McMillan plan was obviously a long-range proposal. While some of the projects, such as the widening and beautification of the Mall and the construction of the pool and Lincoln Memorial, were eventually executed, the monument grounds remained essentially untouched. Plans for the grounds had not been abandoned, however. On the contrary, strong feeling persisted inside and outside of government that if the McMillan plan were to succeed, its plans for the monument grounds would also have to be realized.[54] Nevertheless, the heavy cost of the plan made many in Congress with an eye on austerity hesitant to support it. Two other significant factors also lessened the possibility of completion. One was the question of engineering feasibility—to what extent would the proposed changes affect the monument's stability? A second question, which had been raised under Casey, was how the sunken garden and its related features would interfere with the imposing simplicity and dignity of the structure, characteristics that had gained numerous adherents ever since the monument was completed.

Proponents of the McMillan plan argued that the garden and terraces would not be appendages to the monument, and that they would leave untouched the simple splendor of the obelisk. One supporter said, "Seen from the lower level [i.e., the sunken garden] the Monument gains an additional height of nearly 45 feet, while at the same time nothing is suffered to come so near as to disturb the isolation which the monument demands".[55]

Opponents questioned the engineering feasibility of the project. They reasoned that building the sunken garden would require excavation of a deep and large depression on one side of the monument. The Office of Public Buildings and Public Parks of the National Capital was convinced that this would lighten the load on the foundation on the west side. At the same time, building terraces on the east side of the monument would add weight to the foundation on that side. The two actions together would create an imbalance that would lead to an uneven settlement in the subsoil of the foundation, resulting in injury to the shaft. Lieutenant Colonel Ulysses S. Grant III, Director of the Office of Public Buildings and Public Parks of the National Capital in the 1920s, recommended to Congress that the National Capital Park and Planning Commission, appointed in 1926, be provided with an adequate appropriation to investigate the engineering feasibility of the McMillan plan or a modification. He suggested that the commission hire experts in foundations to conduct borings that would extend to solid rock or solid earth, something that had never been done.[56]

Congress agreed with Grant and appropriated $30,000 to study the feasibility of constructing the garden and terraces according to the

McMillan plan. In May 1930 an advisory committee was appointed consisting of eminent architects and engineers, including Frederick Law Olmsted Jr., and Major Douglas H. Gillette of the Corps of Engineers. After the early construction records of the monument were carefully studied and extensive borings were made around the grounds, the committee uncovered considerable information on the subsoil that had never been clearly evident in the early records. The committee found that the monument rested upon a "stiff" bed of sand and gravel, "underlain with a thick blanket of

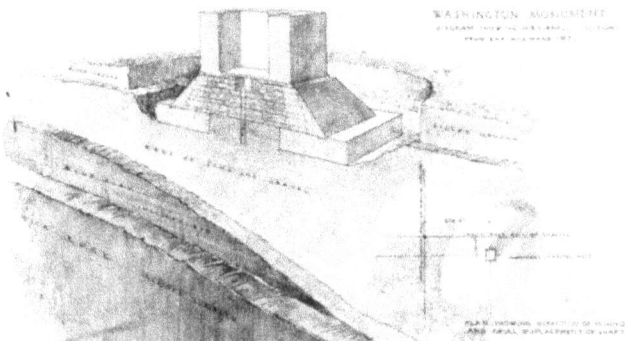

Diagram showing subsurface conditions around the Washington Monument, made from borings done in 1931. *National Archives (National Capitol Planning Commission photograph 328-m-29).*

plastic wet blue clay varying from 20 to 40 feet in thickness." Bedrock was discovered at an average depth of 80 feet below the bottom of the footing. It was also found that the groundwater level rose and fell about .28 of a foot periodically according to the tide in the Potomac River, a level that seemed to be subject to a seasonal variation of as much as 8 feet.

The committee concluded that the McMillan plan would seriously endanger the monument's stability. It reported that there were only two solutions if the McMillan plan were to be implemented, both very costly and unwise. The first was to underpin the monument to bedrock, an extremely difficult approach costing about $600,000. The second alternative was to dismantle the entire monument, constructing a new foundation to bedrock, and rebuild the obelisk, at an estimated cost of $1 million. The committee agreed that without the 1901 plan, the monument was safe in its present condition and no underpinning was necessary. It recommended that the McMillan plan be abandoned as it affected the monument and that other plans, less ambitious, be considered that would bring the monument grounds into harmony with the rest of the Mall.[57]

Two other plans offered at this time were also rejected. Ultimately the whole matter of embellishing the monument grounds was abandoned. In the final analysis, the McMillan plan, which had succeeded in almost every other respect, had failed to realize its most "painstaking and elaborate proposal" for the Washington Monument grounds.[58]

On 10 August 1933, the Washington National Monument was transferred to the control of the National Park Service, ending a long association with the Corps of Engineers that had begun before the Civil War. Thomas Casey had managed completion of the monument; his Engineer successors had preserved and maintained it for nearly a half century. Another fifty years later, it stands still, a monument to the nation's first President and hallmark of the skyline of the city that bears his name.

The monument in 1949. *U.S. Army (photograph SC 315301-NFS).*

Notes

Chapter I

1. Library of Congress, *Journal of the Continental Congress, 1774-1789,* edited by Worthington Chauncey Ford, Gaillard Hunt, John C. Fitzpatrick, and Roscoe R. Hill (Washington: Government Printing Office, 1904-37), XXV, pp. 330, 963.
2. Ibid., XXIV, p. 492.
3. Ibid.
4. "Plan of the City intended for the Permanent Seat of the Government of the United States...on the bank of the Potomac," drawn by Pierre Charles L'Enfant, 1791, copy in the Library of Congress.
5. U.S. Congress, *The Debates and Proceedings in the Congress of the United States with an Appendix containing Important State Papers and Public Documents, and all The Laws of a Public Nature; with a copious Index* (Washington: Gales & Seaton, 1851), 1799, p. 208 (hereafter cited as *Annals of Congress).*
6. Ibid., p. 209.
7. Ibid.
8. Ibid., 1800, p. 708.
9. Ibid., pp. 711-12.
10. Ibid., pp. 800-81.
11. Ibid., p. 801.
12. Ibid., p. 804.
13. Ibid., pp. 818-20.
14. U.S. Congress, House, *Report of Mr. Williams, Committee on the District of Columbia,* H. Rept. 48, 42d Cong., 2d sess., 1872, p. 35 (hereafter cited as H. Rept. 48); U.S. Congress, House, *Report of Mr. Chipman, Select Committee on the Washington National Monument,* H. Rept. 485, 43d Cong., 1st sess., 1874, p. 2 (hereafter cited as H. Rept. 485).
15. One writer said that when the House passed the appropriation, it was so late in the season that the amendments tacked on to the bill in the Senate did not receive the concurrence of the House, and therefore the Senate refused to act on the appropriation. See John B. Ellis, *The Sights and Secrets of the National Capital: A Work Descriptive of Washington City In All Its Various Phases* (New York: United States Publishing Company, 1869), p. 466 (hereafter cited as Ellis).
16. *Annals of Congress,* 16 February 1816, XXIX, pp. 1009-10; ibid., 14 March 1816, pp. 1211-12.
17. *Annals of Congress,* January 1819, XXXIII, pp. 111-12; ibid., February 1819, pp. 228-29; H. Rept. 485, p. 7.
18. *Annals of Congress,* January 1824, XXXXI, pp. 1044-48; also quoted in H. Rept. 48, p. 36.
19. *Register of Debates In Congress* (Washington: Gales & Seaton, 1832), 53: 367-76; ibid., 54: 1782-12.
20. H. Rept. 485, p. 7. The Greenough statue created an artistic scandal in the

Federal City because Greenough's depiction of Washington like the god Zeus, naked to the waist, offended Victorian proprieties.

Chapter II

1. *The National Intelligencer* (Washington, D.C.), 24 September 1833.
2. Ibid.; Constance McLaughlin Green, *Washington, Village and Capital, 1800-1887* (Princeton: Princeton University Press, 1962), p. 170 (hereafter cited as Green, I).
3. Frederick L. Harvey, *History of the Washington Monument and Washington National Monument Society* (Washington: Government Printing Office, 1903), p. 21; also published as U.S. Congress, Senate, S. Document 224, 57th Cong., 2d sess., 1903 (hereafter cited as Harvey).
4. Ibid., pp. 22-3.
5. H. Rept. 485, p. 2; Extract of Minutes of the Washington National Monument Society, 22 February 1839, Brock Collection, Henry E. Huntington Library and Art Gallery, San Marino, California (hereafter cited as Brock Collection).
6. U.S. Congress, House, *Report of the Select Committee on the Washington National Monument,* H. Rept. 94, 32d Cong., 2d sess., 1855, p. 3 (hereafter cited as H. Rept. 94); Harvey, p. 24.
7. H. Rept. 94, p. 3; Harvey, pp. 25, 37-38.
8. Helen Nicolay, *Our Capital on the Potomac* (New York: The Century Co., 1924), p. 494; H. Rept. 48, p. 37; Harvey, p. 35.
9. Ms., ca. 1838, Brock Collection.
10. Resolution of 6 July 1836 by the Board of Managers, Washington National Monument Society, Records of the Washington National Monument Society, Records of the Office of Public Buildings and Grounds, Record Group 42, National Archives (hereafter cited as RG 42, NA); Society and Congressional Publications concerning the Monument and Society, Box 33, RG 42, NA; Harvey, pp. 25-6.
11. Allen Johnson and Dumas Malone, eds., *Dictionary of American Biography* (New York: Charles Scribner's Sons, 1964) (hereafter cited as *D.A.B.*).
12. Society and Congressional Publications concerning the Monument and the Society, Box 33, RG 42, NA; H. Rept. 48, pp. 8, 37. An identical description appears in Harvey, pp. 26-28. A zocle is the lowest member of a column, pedestal, plinth, or wall.
13. H. Rept. 48, p. 8.
14. Ibid.
15. "Robert Mills and The Washington Monument in Baltimore," *The Maryland Historical Magazine,* XXXIV (June 1939), pp. 144-60.
16. Richard Bing, "George Washington's Monument," *Constructor,* LVIII (December 1976), p. 20 (hereafter cited as Bing).
17. Henry van Brunt, *The American Art Review* (1880), p. 9, (hereafter cited as Van Brunt).
18. Talbot Hamlin, *Greek Revival Architecture in America: Being an Account of Important Trends in American Architecture and American Life prior to the War Between the States* (New York: Dover Publications, Inc., 1944), p. 49.
19. Statement to the Nation by George Watterston, 10 December 1838, Brock Collection.
20. Benne and Platt to Washington National Monument Society, Letters Received Concerning Designs for the Monument, RG 42, NA.
21. U.S. Congress, House, *Report of Committee on Public Buildings and Grounds,* H. Rept. 434, 28th Cong., 1st sess., 1844, p. 1; Harvey, pp. 35-7.

22. Brief History of the Washington National Monument, ca. 1880, Society and Congressional Publications concerning the Monument and the Society, Box 33, RG 42, NA; Harvey, p. 46.

23. Certificate, ca. 1848, Brock Collection.

24. Walhelmus Bogart Bryan, *A History of the National Capital: From Its Foundation Through the Period of the Adoption of the Organic Act,* 2 vols. (New York: The Macmillan Company, 1916), II, p. 323; Green, I, p. 171.

25. Brief History of the Washington National Monument, ca. 1880, Society and Congressional Publications concerning the Monument and the Society, Box 33, RG 42, NA.

26. Ibid.; *The Washington National Monument: Views of the Early Patriots Regarding it; Reasons why it should remain on its present site; objects and uses of such structures; an appeal to the people and their representatives* (Washington: Washington National Monument Society, 1871), p. 13.

27. John W. Reps, *Monumental Washington: The Planning and Development of the Capital Center* (Princeton: Princeton University Press, 1967), p. 44 (hereafter cited as Reps); Bing, p. 21; Green, I, p. 172; John Clagett Proctor, *Washington Past and Present: A History,* 4 vols. (New York: Lewis Historical Publishing Company, Inc., 1930), II, p. 545 (hereafter cited as Proctor).

28. Harvey, pp. 42-43.

29. Clark to President, Washington National Monument Society, 28 September 1875, Box 12, RG 42, NA; Drawing of facilities by Fred A. Stuart, ca. 1875, RG 42, Cartographic Division, NA.

30. Articles of Agreement between Building Committee and William Early, ca. 1848, Letters Received Concerning Foundation, etc., 1848-53, RG 42, NA.

31. U.S. Congress, House, Extract from Report of Lieut. J.C. Ives, 10 August 1859, H. Exec. Document 1, Part 8, 45th Cong., 2d sess., 1877.

32. Dougherty to Carbery, 28 June 1853, Letters Received, RG 42, NA.

33. Symington to Mills, 4 December 1848, Robert Mills Collection, Library of Congress, Washington, D.C. (hereafter cited as Robert Mills Collection).

34. Symington to Carbery, 4 August 1849, Letters Received, RG 42, NA.

35. Dougherty to Whittlesey, 30 June 1848, Box 2, RG 42, NA; Employed at the Washington National Monument, Robert Mills Collection; Bing, p. 21; Harvey, p. 48.

36. Bing, p. 21; Time Book, Washington National Monument, April 1849-October 1892, RG 42, NA. A stonecutter working on the Washington Monument in Richmond, Virginia, earned from $2.00 to $2.25 a day in 1851. See Henry Galliger's statement of work, 1 December 1851, Robert Mills Collection.

37. Advertisement of Proposals for Foundation Stone, ca. 1848, RG 42, NA.

38. *The National Intelligencer,* 15 September 1848.

39. Carbery to Whittlesey, 18 January 1853, quoted in Joint Commission on the Construction of the Washington National Monument, *Foundation of the Washington National Monument* (Washington: The Joint Commission, 1877), pp. 47-8, Box 12, RG 42, NA; also quoted in Harvey, p. 47 (hereafter cited as *Foundation*).

40. *The National Intelligencer,* 15 September 1848.

41. Symington to Mills, 22 May 1848; Symington to Watterston, 30 May 1848; Symington to Watterston, 31 May 1848, all in Proceedings and Letters Received Concerning the Foundation, the Cornerstone, and Stone for the Monument, 1848-53, RG 42, NA; Harvey, pp. 43-44.

42. Quotation is from Green, I, p. 172. See also Harvey, p. 46, and Allen Nevins, ed., *The Diary of a President, 1845-1849* (New York: Longmans, Green and Co., 1929), p. 329. President Polk considered that day important enough to include

the events in great detail in his diary. The stone has never been found. One source suggests that when the Corps of Engineers later altered the foundation, it removed or relocated the stone. See Bing, p. 18.

43. *The National Intelligencer,* 15 September 1848.

44. Carbery to Whittlesey, 18 January 1853, *Foundation,* p. 46.

45. Dougherty to Carbery, 25 September 1854, Records of the Secretary, Washington National Monument Society, RG 42, NA.

46. Carbery to Whittlesey, 18 January 1853, U.S. Congress, House, H. Exec. Doc. 1, 45th Cong., 2d sess., 1877, p. 44.

47. Harvey, p. 48; Proctor, II, p. 545.

48. American Medical Association, printed circular by the Committee Appointed to Solicit Funds for a Stone in the Washington Monument, 7 February 1853, in Library of Congress. One such stone which gave the appearance of advertising a business was inscribed as follows: "New York/ Presented By/ Masterton and Smith/ Morgans Marble/ Westchester County." No references were made to George Washington. See C.D. Gedney, *Sketches of Engraved Stone Tablets Contributed to the Washington National Monument* (The author, 17 February 1880), n.p. in Library of Congress.

49. Eckloff to Force, 31 March 1851, Brock Collection.

50. H. Rept. 94, p. 4; Proceedings of the Joint Commission to Construct the Washington National Monument, 12 December 1885, RG 42, NA (hereafter cited as Proceedings of the Joint Commission).

51. U.S. Congress, House, *Report of Mr. Chipman, Select Committee on the Washington Monument,* H. Rept. 79, 42d Cong., 3d sess., 1873, p. 4 (hereafter cited as H. Rept. 79); *The Washington National Monument: Views of the Early Patriots...,* p. 14.

52. Casey to Corcoran, 27 July 1878, Letters Sent (1878-88), vol. I, RG 42, NA; Proceedings of the Joint Commission, 18 December 1884, RG 42, NA.

53. Proceedings of the Joint Commission, 12 December 1885, RG 42, NA; Casey to Newton, Report of Operations for 1884, Letters Sent (1878-88), vol. IV, RG 42, NA.

54. Proceedings of the Joint Commission, 18 December 1884, RG 42, NA; Casey to Corcoran, 27 July 1878, Letters Sent (1878-88), vol. I, RG 42, NA.

Chapter III

1. Statement of the Washington National Monument Society to the U.S. Senate, ca. 1853, Brock Collection.

2. John F. Wershampel, *The Pope's Strategem: Rome to America: An Address to the Protestants of the United States Against Placing the Pope's Block of Marble in the Washington Monument* (Baltimore: 1852), in the Library of Congress; Harvey, p. 53.

3. W.B. Bryan, *A History of the National Capital,* 2 vols. (New York: The Macmillan Co., 1916), II, p. 427.

4. *The National Intelligencer,* Washington, D.C., 8 March 1854, as quoted in Harvey, p. 52. See also J.E. Griffith, *History of the Washington Monument* (Holyoke, Mass.: The author, 1885), pp. 65-69, for a detailed account of the event (hereafter cited as Griffith).

5. H. Rept. 94, p. 5.

6. Newspaper extract, "Washington National Monument Office," 23 February 1855, Brock Collection; Bryan, II, p. 427; Ms., from Secretary Brent of the

Washington National Monument Society, 7 March 1855, Brock Collection; H. Rept. 79, p. 4.

   7. Ms., Charges against the old board, 22 February 1856, Brock Collection.

   8. Bryan, II, p. 427; Bing, p. 22; Helen Nicolay, *Our Capital on the Potomac* (New York: The Century Co., 1924), p. 495.

   9. Harvey, p. 67.

   10. H. Rept. 94, p. 5.

   11. D.A.B.

   12. Extract of a report of Lt. J.C. Ives, 10 August 1859, H. Rept. 48, pp. 3-4.

   13. "Foundations of the Washington National Monument," footnote, p. 2, in Records relating to the Design & Construction of the Monument Grounds and to the Offices of the Society, 1850-90, Records of the Secretary, RG 42, NA; Harvey, pp. 68-69.

   14. Morgan to Brent, 7 May 1861, Box 12, RG 42, NA; Green, I, p. 262; Benjamin Franklin Cooling, *Symbol, Sword, and Shield* (Hampden, Conn.: Archon Books, 1975), p. 49. There is an interesting wood engraving of the scene around the monument grounds during the war in *Frank Leslie's Illustrated,* 1 February 1862, p. 173.

   15. Widdecomb to Secretary of the Washington National Monument Society, 15 December 1884, Records of the Secretary, RG 42, NA.

   16. Albert E. Cowdrey, *A City for the Nation: The Army Engineers and the Building of Washington, D.C., 1790-1967* (Washington: Office of the Chief of Engineers, 1978), p. 27 (hereafter cited as Cowdrey).

   17. Harvey, p. 74.

   18. Ellis, pp. 470-71.

Chapter IV

   1. *The New York Herald,* 1 January 1871; Resolution adopted by the Alexandria and Virginia Marble Company, March 1876, Box 12, RG 42, NA.

   2. Brent to Starkweather, 6 March 1872, H. Rept. 48; H. Rept. 79.

   3. H. Rept. 79.

   4. Chipman to Humphreys, 12 February 1873, *Foundation.*

   5. Lt. Marshall's Report, 19 February 1873, *Foundation,* p. 4; also printed in H. Rept. 79. Biographical data on Lt. Marshall is available at the United States Military Academy, West Point, N.Y.

   6. Ibid., Lt. Marshall's report, 19 February 1873.

   7. H. Rept. 79

   8. H. Rept. 485.

   9. Chipman to Belknap, 24 January 1874, *Foundation.* pp. 7-8.

   10. Note of Major General A.A. Humphreys, 29 January 1874, Records of the Corps of Engineers, Record Group 77, National Archives (hereafter cited as RG 77, NA); Report of Lt. Marshall to Gen. Humphreys, 10 April 1874, H. Rept. 485.

   11. H. Rept. 485; Speech of Hon. John B. Storm, 4 June 1874, in the House of Representatives, *Washington National Monument: Shall the Unfinished Obelisk Stand a Monument of National Disgrace and National Dishonor* (Washington: Government Printing Office, 1874), pp. 14-15.

   12. Harvey, p. 81.

   13. *The New York Tribune,*1 July 1875.

   14. Chipman to Belknap, 26 June 1874, and third indorsement, 6 July 1874, *Foundation,* pp. 20-21.

15. Casey to Board of Engineers for Fortifications, 6 July 1874, *Foundation*, p. 21.
16. Board of Engineers to Humphreys, 7 August 1874, *Foundation*, pp. 22-24.
17. Indorsement of 3 October 1874, *Foundation*.
18. Ada Louise Huxtable, "The Washington Monument, 1836-1884," *Progressive Architecture* (August 1957), p. 142 (hereafter cited as Huxtable).
19. Brief History of the Washington National Monument, ca. 1880, Box 33, RG 42, NA; *United States Statues at Large*, approved 2 August 1876, Chapter 250, p. 123; Harvey, pp. 89-90.
20. Harvey, p. 89.
21. Ibid., p. 88.
22. Proceedings of the Joint Commission, 12 September 1876, RG 42, NA.
23. Ibid., 22 November 1876.
24. U.S. Army Special Order No. 196, 21 September 1876, *Foundation*, p. 26; also printed in U.S. Congress, House, H. Exec. Doc. 1, Part 8, 45th Cong., 2d sess., 1877 (hereafter cited as H. Exec. Doc. 1).
25. Report of the Board of Engineers, 10 April 1877, *Foundation*, pp. 26-38. There is evidence that the board may have prepared a report as early as January 1877 that was rejected by General Humphreys as not containing all the information requested by the Joint Commission's resolution. Lt. Kingman had submitted his findings in late December 1876. See Humphreys to Corcoran, 30 January 1877, General Records, RG 77, NA.
26. Report of the Board of Engineers, 10 April 1877, p. 27.
27. Proceedings of the Joint Commission, 16 April 1877, RG 42, NA.
28. *Analytical Review on the Various Reports of the Washington Monument: Review of the Report of the Board of U.S. Army Engineer on the Foundation of the Washington National Monument by the Washington National Monument Society* (Washington: Gibson Brothers, Printers, 1877), Box 33, RG 42, NA.
29. Blake to Humphreys, 24 April 1877, H. Exec. Doc. 1.
30. Blake to Hayes, 31 May 1877, H. Exec. Doc. 1. Normally, the Society would have addressed its reply to the president of the Joint Commission, but since Corcoran was both president of the commission and an officer of the Society, it was thought best to send it to President Rutherford B. Hayes, also a member of the commission.
31. Extract of U.S. Army Special Order No. 44, 7 May 1877, H. Exec. Doc. 1; Kurtz et al. to Joint Commission, 13 June 1877, ibid.
32. Blake to Hayes, 11 October 1877, H. Exec. Doc. 1.
33. Ibid.
34. The day before the board dispatched this letter, Col. J.D. Kurtz, senior member of the board, died. Duane and Gillmore to Joint Commission, 17 October 1877, H. Exec. Doc. 1.
35. H. Exec. Doc. 1; U.S. Congress, House, 46th Cong., 2d sess., H. Rept. 1107, 1880.
36. Proceedings of the Joint Commission, 22 June 1878, RG 42, NA; U.S. Army Special Order 136, 25 June 1878, Box 12, RG 42, NA. According to the Society's historian, Davis was recommended and endorsed by the Society. See Harvey, p. 96.
37. This biographical sketch is based upon the following works: *D.A.B.* Supplement 1, pp. 156-57; *Webster's American Military Biographies* (Springfield, Mass.: G. & C. Merriam Company, 1978), p. 64; Henry L. Abbott, "Memoir of Thomas Lincoln Casey, 1831-1896," *National Academy of Sciences, Biographical Memoirs* (1902), IV, pp. 125-34 (hereafter cited as Abbott); *Biographical Register of the Officers and Graduates of the U.S. Military Academy at West Point, New York Since Its Establishment in 1802* (Cambridge, Mass., 1901), II, pp. 471-73 and Vol.

IV, pp. 83-84; and Bernard R. Green, "Thomas Lincoln Casey," *Twenty-Seventh Annual Reunion of the Association of the Graduates of the United States Military Academy, at West Point, New York, June 11, 1896* (Saginaw, Mich., 1896), pp. 138-49 (hereafter cited as Green, "Casey").

38. Casey to Corcoran, 25 June 1878, Letters Sent, Vol. I, Records of the Engineer in Charge of Construction, RG 42, NA; Harvey to Hill, 13 November 1879, Log Book, RG 42, NA. Meetings of the Building Committee were held in the Widener Building at the corner of 17th and G Streets NW.

39. Proceedings of the Joint Commission, 27 June 1878, RG 42, NA. In Wright to Casey, 27 July 1878, General Records, RG 77, NA, Lt. Col. Wright, a subordinate of Gen. Humphreys and later his successor, sent all papers and records from the period 1874 to 1877, then in the hands of the Corps, to Casey. Casey to Corcoran, 28 June 1878, Letters Sent, Vol. I, RG 42, NA. It is interesting to note that in November 1879, Casey was permitted a telephone in his office in order to communicate with the monument site, and according to him the value of that connection was demonstrated daily. See Report of Operations for November 1879, Letters Sent, Vol. I, RG 42, NA.

40. Corcoran to Casey, 1 July 1878, Letters Sent, Vol. I, RG 42, NA; U.S. Congress, House, H. Misc. Doc. 7, 45th Cong., 3d sess.,1878 (hereafter cited as H. Misc. Doc. 7).

41. Proceedings of the Joint Commission, 23 October 1878; ibid., 26 October 1878; ibid., 7 December 1878; ibid., 9 January 1879, all in RG 42, NA.

42. Casey to Humphreys, 16 December 1878, Records of the Secretary, RG 42, NA.

43. Humphreys and Clark to Joint Commission, 5 February 1879, Records of the Secretary, RG 42, NA.

44. Proceedings of the Joint Commission, 21 December 1878, citing Corcoran's letter of the same date, RG 42, NA.

45. Hayes to Edwards, 24 December 1886, Charles Richard Williams, *Life of Rutherford Birchard Hayes: Nineteenth President of the United States*, 2 vols. (Boston: Houghton, Mifflin Co., 1914), II, pp. 225-26 (hereafter cited as Williams).

46. Stuart to Corcoran, 20 October 1877, H. Exec. Doc. 1; Casey to Joint Commission, 5 July 1878, Letters Sent, Vol. I, RG 42, NA.

47. Casey to Corcoran, 27 July 1878, Letters Sent, Vol. I, RG 42, NA; H. Misc. Doc. 7.

48. Proceedings of the Joint Commission, 25 September 1878, RG 42, NA; Report of Operations for October 1878, Letters Sent, Vol. I, RG 42, NA.

49. Mills himself had said that his obelisk, shorn of its pantheon, would look like a "stalk of asparagus." Quotations are from Huxtable, p. 142.

50. Ibid.

51. van Brunt, pp. 9, 65.

52. Ibid., p. 59.

53. Extract from the Proceedings of the Washington National Monument Society at a meeting held on the 17th of December 1878, Records of the Secretary, RG 42, NA.

54. Proceedings of the Joint Commission, 21 December 1878, RG 42, NA.

55. Ibid., 9 January 1879.

56. Winthrop to Morrill, 1 August 1878, printed in Harvey, pp. 302-4.

57. Casey to Humphreys, 23 January 1879, Letters Sent, Vol. I, RG 42, NA. The published version of this letter appears in U.S. Congress, House, H. Misc. Doc. 7, Part 2, 45th Cong., 3d sess., 1879 (hereafter cited as H. Misc. Doc. 7, Part 2).

58. Ibid.; Proceedings of the Joint Commission, 8 February 1879, RG 42, NA;

Corcoran to Congress, 11 February 1879, Letters Sent, Vol. I, RG 42, NA; U.S. Congress, House, H. Rept. 1107, 46th Cong., 2d sess., 1880.

59. Casey to Corcoran, 27 July 1878, Letters Sent, Vol. I, RG 42, NA; H. Misc. Doc. 7, Part 2.

60. Edmunds to Casey, 31 March 1879, with extracts of letters, Marsh to Edmunds, 9 February 1879, and Marsh to Edmunds, 25 April 1879, published in Harvey, pp. 299-302.

61. Marsh to Edmunds, 9 February 1879, U.S. Congress, House, 46th Cong., 2d sess., H. Misc. Doc. 37, 1880 (hereafter cited as H. Misc. Doc. 37); *The Washington Monument* (Washington: The Society of American Military Engineers, 1923), pp. 9-10.

62. Proceedings of the Joint Commission, 17 July 1879, RG 42, NA; Casey to Wright, 8 July 1879, Letters Sent, Vol. I, RG 42, NA.

63. Casey to Winthrop, 19 April 1880, Letters Sent, Vol. II, RG 42, NA. This letter is also printed in U.S. Congres, House, H. Misc. Doc. 37, 1880.

64. H. Misc. Doc. 37.

65. Obituary of Robert C. Winthrop, *The Washington Post*, 22 November 1894.

66. Hayes to Edwards, 24 December 1886, Williams, II, pp. 225-26.

67. Campbell to Brownwell, 12 April 1907, file 48, General Correspondence, 1907-1971, RG 42, NA.

Chapter V

1. The shop for carpenters and riggers was a wooden shelter 28 by 60 feet; a shelter for storing stone was 24 by 100 feet; a smith shop was 24 by 37 feet. These structures were all one-story high. Casey to Corcoran, 2 October 1878, Log Book, RG 42, NA; Report of Operations for October 1878; Casey to Corcoran, 2 December 1878, both in Letters Sent, Vol. I, RG 42, NA.

2. Reports of Operations for October and November 1878 and September 1879, Letters Sent, Vol. I, RG 42, NA; Bill for lumber for stonecutters shed, 4 November 1878, Letters Sent, Vol. I, RG 42, NA.

3. Casey to Wright, 10 January 1880, Letters Sent, Vol. II, RG 42, NA.

4. Report of Operations for July 1878, Letters Sent, Vol. I, RG 42, NA.

5. Reports of Operations for October, November, and December 1878, Letters Sent, Vol. I, RG 42, NA; Casey to Corcoran, 2 December 1878, Letters Sent, Vol. I, RG 42, NA, also printed in H. Misc. Doc. 7; Casey to Wright, 1 December 1879, Letters Sent, Vol. I, RG 42, NA, also printed in U.S. Congress, Senate, 46th Cong., 2d sess., S. Misc. Doc. 7, 1879 (hereafter cited as S. Misc. Doc. 7).

6. Davis to Delameter Iron Works, 13 September 1878, Letters Sent, Vol. I, RG 42, NA.

7. Green to Ward, 13 June 1887, Letters Sent, Vol. IV, RG 42, NA.

8. Casey to Wright, 1 December 1879, Letters Sent, Vol. I, RG 42, NA, also printed in S. Misc. Doc. 7.

9. Report of Operations for September 1879; Casey to Wright, 1 December 1879, both in Letters Sent, Vol. I, RG 42, NA.

10. Reports of Operations for November and December 1878, Letters Sent, Vol. I, RG 42, NA.

11. Davis to J.B. White and Bros., 23 August 1879; Casey's Memorandum, ca. April 1879; Reports of Operations for June and August 1879, all in Letters Sent, Vol. I, RG 42, NA.

12. Specifications for White Marble in the construction of the Washington Monument, ca. 1882, Letters Sent, Vol. III, RG 42, NA.

13. Casey to Gillmore, 6 December 1878; Reports of Operations for November and December 1878, all in Letters Sent, Vol. I, RG 42, NA.

14. Report of Operations for August 1879, Letters Sent, Vol. I, RG 42, NA.

15. Casey to Briggs, 9 January 1880, Letters Sent, Vol. I, RG 42, NA.

16. Casey to Wright, 1 December 1880, Letters Sent, Vol. II, RG 42, NA; Casey to Wright, 3 April 1883, Letters Sent, Vol. III, RG 42, NA.

17. Casey to Sisson, 1 December 1880, Letters Sent, Vol. II; Proceedings of the Joint Commission, 6 December 1880, both in RG 42, NA.

18. Casey to Wright, 3 April 1883; Casey to Wright, 27 June 1883, both in Letters Sent, Vol. III, RG 42, NA.

19. Proceedings of the Joint Commission, 12 December 1883, RG 42, NA.

20. Specifications of Granite required in the construction of the Washington Monument in the city of Washington, D.C., ca. 1882, Letters Sent, Vol. III, RG 42, NA.

21. A contract with Davis Tillson of Rockland, Maine, was signed in July 1880. See Casey to Wright, 1 December 1880. A contract with the Cape Ann Granite Company was signed in 1881. See Report of Operations for July 1881, both in Letters Sent, Vol. II, RG 42, NA. A contract with the Bodwell Granite Company was signed in May 1882. See Report of Operations for May 1882, Letters Sent, Vol. III, RG 42, NA.

22. Casey to Wright, 1 December 1879, Letters Sent, Vol. I, RG 42, NA; also printed in U.S. Congress, Senate, S. Misc. Doc. 17, 1879.

23. Report of Operations for July 1878, Letters Sent, Vol. I, RG 42, NA.

24. Casey to Chief Engineer, Sutro Tunnel, 6 September 1878, Letters Sent, Vol. I, RG 42, NA.

25. Report of Operations for September 1878, Letters Sent, Vol. I, RG 42, NA.

26. Return of Officers and Men for February 1879; Report of Operations for September 1879, both in Letters Sent, Vol. I, RG 42, NA.

27. Casey to Wright, 10 June 1880, Letters Sent, Vol. II, RG 42, NA.

28. Reports of Operations for July, August, and September 1880, all in Letters Sent, Vol. I, RG 42, NA; Report of Operations for September 1882, Letters Sent, Vol. III, RG 42, NA.

29. Davis to Murch, 22 September 1880, Letters Sent, Vol. II, RG 42, NA. Casey wired the same congressman, "Five men sent on by you have been or will be employed. There is no room for any more." Casey to Murch, 22 September 1880, Letters Sent, Vol. II, RG 42, NA.

30. Report of Operations for May 1881, Letters Sent, Vol. II, RG 42, NA.

31. Report of Operations for January 1883, Letters Sent, Vol. III; Casey to Wright, 25 March 1881, Letters Sent, Vol. II; Wright to Casey, 28 March 1881, Log Book, all in RG 42, NA.

32. Entry 465 in Inventory, Time Book, Washington National Monument, April 1849 to 1892, RG 42, NA.

33. Report of Operations for August 1880, Letters Sent, Vol. I, RG 42, NA; Griffith p. 13.

34. Casey to Newton, 14 May 1884, Letters Sent, Vol. III; Casey to Lawrence, 14 November 1884, Letters Sent, Vol. IV, both in RG 42, NA.

35. Davis to Casey, 6 September 1884, Letters Sent, Vol. III, RG 42, NA.

36. Brief History of the Washington National Monument, ca. 1880, Ms. in Box 33; Proceedings of the Joint Commission, 18 December 1884, both in RG 42, NA.

37. Casey to Winthrop, 19 April 1880, Letters Sent, Vol. II, RG 42, NA.

38. Casey to Wright, 1 December 1879, Letters Sent, Vol. I; Proceedings of the Joint Commission, 18 December 1884; Brief History of the Washington National Monument, ca. 1880, Ms. in Box 33, all in RG 42, NA.

39. Casey to Wright, 15 October and 1 December 1879, Letters Sent, Vol. I; Proceedings of the Joint Commission, 21 October 1879, both in RG 42, NA.

40. Report of Operations for October 1879, Letters Sent, Vol. I; Report of Operations for May 1880, Letters Sent, Vol. II, both in RG 42, NA.

41. Casey to Wright, 1 December 1880, Letters Sent, Vol. II; Wright to Casey, 13 December 1880, Log Book; Reports of Operations for January and February 1881, Letters Sent, Vol. II; Casey to Wright, 10 December 1881, Letters Sent, Vol. III, all in RG 42, NA.

42. As quoted in Myrtle Cheney Murdock, *Your Memorials In Washington* (Washington: Monumental Press, Inc., 1952), p. 170.

43. Casey to Wright, 1 December 1880, Letters Sent, Vol. II, RG 42, NA.

44. Ibid.

45. Casey to Chairman, Building Committee, 3 June 1879, Letters Sent, Vol. I, RG 42, NA.

46. Ibid.

47. Casey to Otis Brothers and Co., 20 August 1879, Letters Sent, Vol. I, RG 42, NA. Because of the highly technical nature of this ironwork and because of the extreme height this framework was to reach, Casey took great care to instruct the contractors on the preparation of every piece of iron that was to be supplied and installed. See "Description of Iron Work Construction projecting above masonry, Washington Monument, and Apparatus for hoisting and setting stone," n.d., Letters Sent, Vol. II, RG 42, NA.

48. Ibid.; U.S. Congress, Senate, S. Misc. Doc. No. 17, 1879; Report of Operations for November 1879, Letters Sent, Vol. I, RG 42, NA.

49. Casey to Wright, 1 December 1879; Report of Operations for November 1879, both in Letters Sent, Vol. I, RG 42, NA; Report of Operations for December 1879, Letters Sent, Vol. II, RG 42, NA.

50. Casey to Wright, 1 December 1880, Letters Sent, Vol. II, RG 42, NA.

51. Casey to Wright, 7 May 1880; Casey to Wright, 1 December 1880, both in Letters Sent, Vol. II, RG 42, NA.

52. Washington Monument Plan of Masonry at Ref. 150 ft., signed by Casey, ca. 1880, Records of the National Park Service, Record Group 79, Cartographic Division, National Archives.

53. Casey to Wright, 1 December 1880, Letters Sent, Vol. II, RG 42, NA; Harvey, pp. 98-99.

54. Casey to Wright, 1 December 1880, Letters Sent, Vol. II, RG 42, NA. Just before work on the new addition began, Casey recommended to the Building Committee that he use Portland cement mortar in setting the new ashler marble. He also suggested using hydraulic lime of teil in pointing the exterior joints. Portland cement (one part cement and two parts sand) was also proposed for setting the granite. See entry in Log Book, 3 August 1880, and Brief History of the Washington National Monument, ca. 1880, Ms. in Box 33, Records of the Secretary, both in RG 42, NA. Casey also proposed that this procedure be used in the Bunker Hill Monument. Casey to Darracott, 18 July 1882, Letters Sent, Vol. III, RG 42, NA.

55. Casey to Wright, 10 December 1881, Letters Sent, Vol. III, RG 42, NA; also printed in U.S. Congress, Senate, Misc. Doc. No. 19, 47th Cong., 1st sess., 1881.

56. Ibid.

57. Although Casey had requested $200,000 the year before, he was only given $150,000 in the last appropriation. By the end of 1882, he had a balance of only $33,417 on hand after expenditures. See footnote.

58. Casey to Wright, 21 December 1882, Letters Sent, Vol. III, RG 42, NA; also printed in U.S. Congress, Senate, Misc. Doc. 13, 47th Cong., 2d sess., 1882.

59. Casey to Wright, 6 December 1883, Letters Sent, Vol. III, RG 42, NA; also

printed in U.S. Congress, Senate, Misc. Doc. 22, 48th Cong., 1st sess., 1883.
60. Ibid.
61. Ibid.
62. Casey to Newton, 18 December 1884, Letters Sent, Vol. IV, RG 42, NA. Brig. Gen. John Newton had replaced Gen. Wright as Chief of Engineers and Chairman of the Building Committee of the Joint Commission. Also printed in U.S. Congress, House, Misc. Doc. 8, 48th Cong., 2nd sess.,1884.
63. Casey to Corcoran, 27 July 1878, Letters Sent, Vol. I, RG 42, NA; also printed in H. Misc. Doc. 7, Part 2.
64. O.H. Tittman, et al., "Memoir of Bernard Richardson Green," *Transactions of the American Society of Civil Engineers* (December 1916), LXXX, pp. 2151-56 (hereafter cited as Tittman); Cowdrey, p. 28.
65. *The Washington Monument* (Washington: The Society of American Military Engineers, 1923), p. 9. Following his assignment as aide to Gen. Sheridan, Davis was appointed military governor of Puerto Rico in 1899-1900. In 1900 he was promoted to colonel and in 1901 to brigadier general in the Regular Army. After he retired from active duty in 1903, he was appointed a member of the Isthmian Canal Commission by President Theodore Roosevelt. Davis later became governor of the Canal Zone, where he organized a new government before retiring from office in 1905. Thereafter he went on two special diplomatic missions to Guatemala. He died on 12 July 1918.
66. Green, "Casey," pp. 143-44. Green's biographer gives him the credit for designing the pyramidion. See Tittmann, p. 2152.
67. "Washington Monument. Project for a Marble Pyramidion, January 19, 1884," Sheet No. 1, RG 79, Cartographic Branch, NA.
68. Harvey, p. 96.
69. Casey to Wright, 19 January 1884, Letters Sent, Vol. III, RG 42, NA; Log Book of the Building Committee, 6 February 1884; Proceedings of the Joint Commission, 11 February 1884, all in RG 42, NA.
70. Reports of Operations for May, July, and August 1884, Letters Sent, Vol. III, RG 42, NA.
71. Reports of Operations for September, October, and November 1884, Letters Sent, Vol. IV, RG 42, NA.
72. Casey to Mordecai, 15 June 1885, Letters Sent, Vol. IV, RG 42, NA.
73. Harvey, p. 295; Report of Operations for December 1884; Casey to Frishmuth, 29 October 1884, both in Letters Sent, Vol. IV, RG 42, NA.
74. Report of Operations for December 1884, Letters Sent, Vol. IV, RG 42, NA; Harvey, pp. 99-100. One witness provides a detailed account of this occasion and a good description of the aluminum point. See Griffith, pp. 9-13.
75. Griffith, pp. 15-16.
76. Casey to Poole and Hunt, 11 December 1884, with specifications enclosed, Letters Sent, Vol. IV, RG 42, NA. Quotation is from Casey to Newton, 8 December 1885, Letters Sent, Vol. IV, RG 42, NA; also printed in U.S. Congress, Senate, S. Exec. Doc. 6, 49th Cong., 1st sess., 1885 (hereafter cited as S. Exec. Doc. 6).
77. Report of Operations for March 1885; Casey to Newton, 18 December 1884, both in Letters Sent, Vol. IV, RG 42, NA; Proceedings of the Joint Commission, 18 December 1884; *Roose's Companion and Guide to Washington and Vicinity* (Washington: Gibson Brothers, Printers, 1887), p. 111.
78. Proceedings of the Joint Commission, 16 April 1884, RG 42, NA.
79. Report of Operations for January 1885; Casey to Newton, 8 December 1885, both in Letters Sent, Vol. IV, RG 42, NA.
80. Ben Perley Poore, *Perley's Reminiscences of Sixty Years In the National Metropolis,* 2 vols. (Philadelphia: Hubbard Brothers, Pub., 1886), II, p. 472; Myrtle

Cheney Murdock, *Your Memorials In Washington* (Washington: Monument Press, Inc., 1952), pp. 168-70.

Chapter VI

1. Casey to Wright, 8 March 1883, Letters Sent, Vol. III, RG 42, NA.
2. Proceedings of the Joint Commission, 18 December 1884, RG 42, NA. Nearly all the work would be done by contract under Casey's supervision. Casey to Newton, 10 December 1885, Letters Sent, Vol. IV, RG 42, NA.
3. Casey to Newton, 18 December 1884, Letters Sent, Vol. IV, RG 42, NA.
4. Proceedings of the Joint Commission, 18 December 1884, RG 42, NA.
5. Specifications for Wrought and Cast Iron Work required in completing the stairs, platforms and Elevator fronts inside the Washington Monument, ca. 1885; Casey to Newton, 8 December 1885; Report of Operations for February 1886, all in Letters Sent, Vol. IV, RG 42, NA.
6. Casey to Duane, 20 December 1886; Report of Operations for August 1886, both in Letters Sent, Vol. IV, RG 42, NA.
7. Proceedings of the Joint Commission, 24 April 1882; Proceedings of the Joint Commission, 18 December 1884, both in RG 42, NA.
8. Casey to Newton, 8 April 1885, Letters Sent, Vol. IV, RG 42, NA.
9. Reports of Operations for June, July, August, and December 1885, Letters Sent, Vol. IV, RG 42, NA; Casey to Newton, 8 December 1885, Letters Sent, Vol. IV, RG 42, NA; also printed in S. Exec. Doc. 6.
10. Casey to Newton, 8 December 1885, Letters Sent, Vol. IV; Proceedings of the Joint Commission, 12 December 1885, both in RG 42, NA; S. Exec. Doc. 6.
11. S. Exec. Doc. 6.
12. Quotation is from Casey to Duane, 20 December 1886, Letters Sent, Vol. IV, RG 42, NA; Abbott, p. 134.
13. Casey to Newton, 8 December 1885, Letters Sent, Vol. IV, RG 42, NA; also printed in S. Exec. Doc. 6; Report of Operations for January 1885, Letters Sent, Vol. IV; Proceedings of the Joint Commission, 18 December 1884; Casey to Duane, 20 December 1886, Letters Sent, Vol. IV, all in RG 42, NA.
14. Newton to War Department, 2 June 1885, General Records, Records of the Corps of Engineers, Record Group 77, National Archives; Report of Operations for January 1887, Letters Sent, Vol. IV, RG 42, NA; Custodian to Wilson, 9 May 1894, Letters Received, Box 14, RG 42, NA.
15. Proceedings of the Joint Commission, 18 December 1884; Casey to Newton, 8 April 1885, Letters Sent, Vol. IV, both in RG 42, NA.
16. Casey to Duane, 20 December 1886, Letters Sent, Vol. IV, RG 42, NA.
17. Report of Operations for September 1878, Letters Sent, Vol. I, RG 42, NA.
18. *The American Architect and Building News*, 10 July 1880, VIII, p. 237; ibid., 11 September 1880, VIII, p. 122.
19. Casey to Wright, 5 November 1880, Letters Sent, Vol. II; Proceedings of the Joint Commission, 6 December 1880; Casey to Newton, 8 December 1885, Letters Sent, Vol. IV, all in RG 42, NA; also printed in S. Exec. Doc. 6.
20. Casey to Newton, 8 December 1885; Specifications for inserting memorial stones, ca. 1885; Reports of Operations for June and September 1885, all in Letters Sent, Vol. IV, RG 42, NA; S. Exec. Doc. 6.
21. Wilson to Thomas, 31 July 1888; Wilson to Chief of Engineers, 4 October 1888, both in Letters Sent, Vol. V, RG 42, NA; U.S. Congress, Senate, S. Doc. 332, 71st Cong., 3d sess. Also published as H. Paul Caemmerer, *Washington: The Na-*

tional Capital (Washington: Government Printing Office, 1932), p. 295 (hereafter cited as Caemmerer).

22. Proceedings of the Joint Commission, 29 March 1882, RG 42, NA.
23. Casey to Corcoran, 20 April 1882, Letters Sent, Vol. III, RG 42, NA.
24. Proceedings of the Joint Commission, 24 April 1882, RG 42, NA.
25. Proceedings of the Joint Commission, 18 December 1884, RG 42, NA, also printed in U.S. Congress, House, H. Misc. Doc. 8, 48th Cong., 2d sess., 1884 (hereafter cited as H. Misc. Doc. 8); Griffith, p. 73.
26. Proceedings of the Joint Commission, 18 December 1884, RG 42, NA; also printed in H. Misc. Doc. 8; Casey to Duane, 17 November 1886, Letters Sent, Vol. IV, RG 42, NA.
27. Casey to Duane, 17 November 1886, Letters Sent, Vol. IV, RG 42, NA.
28. Proceedings of the Joint Commission, 22 December 1886; Reports of Operations for March and June 1887, Letters Sent, Vol. IV; Proceedings of the Joint Commission, 17 December 1887, all in RG 42, NA: U.S. Congress, Senate, S. Misc. Doc. 22, 50th Cong., 1st sess., 1887.
29. Proctor, II, p. 546.
30. Joseph West Moore, *Picturesque Washington: Pen and Pencil Sketches* (Providence: J.A. and R.A. Reid, 1887), p. 65.
31. Casey to Duane, 20 December 1886, Letters Sent, Vol. IV; Proceedings of the Joint Commission, 22 December 1886, both in RG 42, NA.
32. Corcoran to Carlisle, 8 January 1887, Copies of Letters Sent, 1876-1888, pp. 197-202, RG 42, NA.
33. Report of Operations for March 1887; Green to Mussey, 30 April 1887; Casey to Duane, 4 May 1887, all in Letters Sent, Vol. IV, RG 42, NA; Proceedings of the Joint Commission, 7 May 1887, RG 42, NA.
34. Report of Operations for period 1 to 9 April 1888, Letters Sent, Vol. IV. This was Casey's last report to the Building Committee. Report of Operations for April 1888, Letters Sent, Vol. V, both reports in RG 42, NA. Special Order No. 76, Army A.G.O., Washington, 3 April 1888, appointed Wilson. See *Annual Report of the Chief of Engineers, U.S. Army, for Fiscal Year 1922,* Report of the Officer in Charge of Public Buildings and Grounds, p. 2198.
35. U.S. Congress, Senate, S. Misc. Doc. 142, 50th Cong., 1st sess., 1888; Report of Operations for September 1888, Letters Sent, Vol. V, RG 42, NA; *Annual Report of the Chief of Engineers, U.S. Army, for Fiscal Year 1890,* Appendix AAA, Report of the Officer in Charge of Public Buildings and Grounds, p. 2829.
36. *The American Architect and Building News,* 9 August 1884, XVI, p. 61.
37. *The American Architect and Building News,* 13 December 1884, XVI, p. 277.
38. Henry O. Avery, "The Washington Monument," *The American Architect and Building News,* 13 December 1884, XVI, pp. 468-69. One later critic observed: "There is no doubt but that the present condition looks somewhat unfinished and incomplete, and it is reasonable to expect that such a structure should appear to rest upon something more than the bare ground as it stands today." See *Proctor, II,* p. 489. Robert Mills' biographer decried the absence of a base of Mills' proportions; even a modified pantheon would be better than none. See H.M. Pierce Gallagher, *Robert Mills: Architect of the Washington Monument, 1781-1855* (New York: Columbia University Press, 1935, reprinted by AMS Press Inc., 1966), p. 124. Another critic was convinced that the base should be surrounded by a Grecian temple containing in the interior crypts for 24 generals and 24 admirals. See Falcon to Superintendent of Government Grounds, 16 March 1891, Letters Received, Box 4, RG 42, NA.
39. Griffith, p. 20.

40. Caemmerer, p. 297; also published in U.S. Congress, Senate, S. Doc. 332, 71st Cong., 3d sess., 1932.
    41. Quoted in Reps, pp. 120-21.
    42. Talbot Hamlin, *Greek Revival Architecture in America: Being an Account of Important Trends in American Architecture and American Life prior to The War Between the States* (New York: Dover Publications, Inc., 1944), p. 49.

Chapter VII

1. *Annual Report of the Chief of Engineers, U.S. Army, for Fiscal Year 1922,* Report of the Officer in Charge of Public Buildings and Grounds, p. 2197 (hereafter cited as *Annual Report of the Chief of Engineers); Annual Report of the Chief of Engineers for FY 1923,* p. 2045.
    2. *Annual Report of the Chief of Engineers for FY 1890,* p. 2829; Miscellaneous ms., RG 42, NA.
    3. Wilson to Wise, 3 October 1888, Letters Sent, Vol. V; Washington National Monument Log Book, containing List of Employees, both in RG 42, NA.
    4. Ibid.
    5. Wilson to Casey, 1 June 1894, Press Copies of Letters Sent, Vol. 66t, RG 42, NA.
    6. Custodian to Bingham, 18 July 1902, Letters, 1899-1906, File 1407, RG 42, NA.
    7. Report of Operations for September 1886, Letters Sent, Vol. IV; Proceedings of the Joint Commission, 7 May 1887, both in RG 42, NA.
    8. *Annual Report of the Chief of Engineers for FY 1889,* p. 3387; *Annual Report of the Chief of Engineers for FY 1899,* p. 3818; *Annual Report of the Chief of Engineers for FY 1914,* p. 3360.
    9. *Annual Report of the Chief of Engineers for FY 1915,* p. 3728.
    10. The Washington National Monument Log Book, "Number of Visitors to Monument from October 1, 1915, to February 11, 1923," RG 42, NA; *Annual Report of the Director of Public Buildings and Public Parks of the National Capital for FY 1931,* p. 87.
    11. *Annual Report of the Chief of Engineers for FY 1893,* p. 4317; *Annual Report of the Chief of Engineers for FY 1899,* p. 3818; *Annual Report of the Chief of Engineers for FY 1895,* p. 4131.
    12. Congressman, First District of Colorado, to Custodian, 18 December 1893, Letters Received, Box 13, RG 42, NA.
    13. Poole to Ridley, 30 April 1919, with three indorsements, General Correspondence 1907-21, File 48, RG 42, NA.
    14. Butterworth to Custodian, 20 May 1892, Letters Received, Box 8; Memorandum, 28 April 1893, Letters Received, Box 10, both in RG 42, NA.
    15. *Annual Report of the Chief of Engineers for FY 1897,* p. 4033.
    16. *Annual Report of the Chief of Engineers for FY 1924,* p. 2034.
    17. *Annual Report of the Chief of Engineers for FY 1915,* p. 3728; *Annual Report of the Director of Public Buildings and Public Parks of the National Capital for FY 1927,* p. 15.
    18. *Annual Report of the Chief of Engineers for FY 1923,* p. 2045.
    19. *Annual Report of the Chief of Engineers for FY 1905,* pp. 2629-30.
    20. *Annual Report of the Chief of Engineers for FY 1890,* p. 2829; *Annual Report of the Chief of Engineers for FY 1905,* p. 2628.
    21. *Annual Report of the Chief of Engineers for FY 1904,* p. 3909; Design for a new Guard rail, 23 June 1927, Cartographic Division, Records of the National Park Service, Record Group 79, National Archives.

22. *Annual Report of the Director of Public Buildings and Public Parks of the National Capital for 1931,* pp. 86-7.

23. Casey to Newton, 8 December 1885, Letters Sent, Vol. IV, RG 42, NA.

24. Proceedings of the Joint Commission, 12 December 1885; Corcoran to Dibble, 5 January 1886, Log Book; "An Act," ca. 1886, Letters Sent, Vol. IV, all in RG 42, NA.

25. Report of Operations for September 1886, Letters Sent, Vol. IV; Corcoran to Dibble, 18 February 1887, Copies of Letters Sent and Received 1876-88, Records of the Joint Commission for the Completion of the Washington Monument, both in RG 42, NA.

26. Rules and Regulations in connection with the Washington Monument, 1 May 1890, Letters Received (1891), Box 6, RG 42, NA; Rules and Regulations in connection with the Washington Monument, 30 July 1907, General Correspondence 1907-21, File 48, RG 42, NA.

27. U.S. Attorney General to Secretary of War, 24 August 1895, Letters Received, Box 20, RG 42, NA.

28. Wilson to Thomas, 18 April 1888, Letters sent, Vol. V, RG 42, NA.

29. *Annual Report of the Chief of Engineers for FY 1889,* p. 3387.

30. Proceedings of the Joint Commission, 7 May 1887, RG 42, NA.

31. Toner to Ernst, 16 June 1890, with indorsement, Casey to Proctor, 16 June 1890, Letters Received, in brown envelope, RG 42, NA. According to Horatio King, a leading member of the Society during this period and one of those who opposed hanging the plaque, the tablet cost $1,300, money that he felt the Society should have turned over to the government to help maintain the monument. King to Wilson, 17 April 1896, Letters Received, 1889-98, RG 42, NA.

32. Proctor to Society, 24 June 1890, Letters Received, in brown envelope, RG 42, NA.

33. Bingham to Wilson, 13 September 1898, Press Copies of Letters Sent, Vol. 87, RG 42, NA.

34. Statement of Col. Theodore A. Bingham, Officer in Charge of Public Buildings and Grounds, 30 September 1901, Letters Received, 1899-1906, RG 42, NA.

35. Proceedings of the Joint Commission, 18 December 1884; Casey to Newton, 8 April 1885, Letters sent, Vol. IV, both in RG 42, NA.

36. "Washington Monument Dying," ca. 1907, news clipping in General Correspondence, 1907-21, File 48, RG 42, NA.

37. Cosby to Obelisk Water Proofing Company, 6 June 1910; Obelisk Water Proofing Company to Cosby, 9 June 1910, both in Public Building and Grounds Correspondence, 1907-21, Metal Box 35, RG 42, NA.

38. *Annual Report of the Director of Public Buildings and Public Parks of the National Capital for 1931,* p. 87.

39. Wilson to Thomas, 16 March 1889, Letters sent, Vol. IX, RG 42, NA. In February 1891, after one of these inspections, the Otis Brothers and Company recommended that the cables be replaced "as soon as possible," since they had been on the elevator a long time. From the time it was inspected two months before "one of the cables, has shown considerable signs of wear." The company suggested that they be changed "at once." Otis Brothers and Company to Ernst, 27 February 1891, Letters Received, Box 4, RG 42, NA. See also *Annual Report of the Chief of Engineers for FY 1890,* p. 2829.

40. *Annual Report of the Chief of Engineers for FY 1893,* p. 4316.

41. Brown *et al.* to Bingham, 3 March 1898, Letters Received, 1889-98, RG 42, NA.

42. Bingham to Brown *et al.,* 15 March 1898, Press Copies of Letters Sent, Vol.

85, RG 42, NA.

43. *Annual Report of the Chief of Engineers for FY 1899,* p. 3819. In a letter to Congressman Lucius N. Littauer, the Sprague Elevator Company, which was interested in installing the electric elevator, expressed the same concerns about the steam elevator while extolling the virtues of an electric one. Besides being more economical and more efficient, the electric elevator would be safer because the chances of mechanical failures would be minimized. This company summed up the advantages of an electric elevator by stressing the compactness of the plant, the simplicity of the plant and its operation, and savings in space, repairs, and fuel. Finally, noted this company, the electric elevator had the ability to make the round trip in at least half the time that was then possible. See Sprague Elevator Company to Littauer, 30 January 1900, Letters Received, 1899-1906, Box 37, RG 42, NA. The Superintendent of the State, War, and Navy Building also agreed that installing the electric elevator system at the monument would "produce the most economical drive in Washington." "It is plain," said the superintendent, "that your plan would pay for itself in 19 months." See Baird to Bingham, 14 April 1900, Letters Received, 1899-1906, Box 37, RG 42, NA.

44. *Annual Report of the Chief of Engineers for FY 1905,* pp. 2629, 2631.

45. Ibid.

46. *Annual Report of the Chief of Engineers for FY 1925,* p. 2629; *Annual Report of the Director of Public Buildings and Public Parks of the National Capital for 1926,* p. 14.

47. Proceedings of the Joint Commission, 8 January 1887; Proceedings of the Joint Commission, 7 May 1887, both in RG 42, NA.

48. Casey to Poindexter and Company, 8 June 1887, Letters Sent, Vol. IV; Proceedings of the Joint Commission, 17 December 1887; Proceedings of the Joint Commission, 10 September 1887; Report of Operations for May 1888, Letters Sent, Vol. V; Report of Operations for September 1888, Letters Sent, Vol. V, all in RG 42, NA.

49. Reports of Operations for July, August, and September 1888, Letters sent, Vol. V, RG 42, NA; Wilson to Sherman, 22 January 1889, Records of the Secretary, Records of the Washington National Monument Society, Box 12, RG 42, NA. There was no transfer of deed, but only a letter from the Society to the Secretary of War turning over the lodge. Bingham to Wilson, 13 September 1898, Press Copies of Letters Sent, Vol. 87, RG 42, NA.

50. *Annual Report of the Chief of Engineers for FY 1889,* pp. 3387-88; *Annual Report of the Chief of Engineers for FY 1890,* p. 2830; *Annual Report of the Chief of Engineers for FY 1891,* p. 3538; *Annual Report of the Chief of Engineers for FY 1892,* pp. 3908-9.

51. *Annual Report of the Chief of Engineers for FY 1893,* p. 4317.

52. U.S. Congress, Senate, S. Rept. 166, 57th Cong., 1st sess., 1902, published as Charles Moore, ed., *The Improvement of the Park System of the District of Columbia* (Washington: Government Printing Office, 1902), Vol. III.

53. Ibid.

54. See, for examle, Charles Moore, *Washington, Past and Present* (New York: The Century Co., 1929), pp. 201-3. Moore was one of the most active supporters of the McMillan plan.

55. Caemmerer, p. 99.

56. "Improvement of the Base and Grounds of the Washington Monument: Hearing before The Committee on The Library," H.R. 11208, A Bill to Provide for Engineering and Landscape Study...the Base and Grounds of the Washington Monument..., U.S. Congress, House, 17th Cong., 1st sess., May 1928; Reps, p. 176.

57. "Improvement of the Washington Monument Grounds," U.S. Congress, House, H. Doc. 528, 72nd Cong., 2d sess., 1933.

58. Frederick Gutheim, *Worthy of the Nation: The History of Planning for the National Capital* (Washington: Smithsonian Institution, 1977), p. 201.

BIBLIOGRAPHY

Manuscripts

San Marino, California. Henry E. Huntington Library and Art Gallery. Brook Collection, 1833-67. This collection consists of 85 manuscripts on the Washington National Monument Society's early involvement with the design and construction of the monument.

Washington, D.C. The Library of Congress. Robert Mills Collection, 1804-62. This collection, consisting of two volumes and one box, contains some information on the monument, but unfortunately very little on the details of Mills' plan and the early years of construction.

Washington, D.C. National Archives and Records Service. Records of the Office of Public Buildings and Grounds. Records of the Washington National Monument Society, 1833-1951. Record Group 42. Consisting of 28 linear feet, this collection represents by far the bulk of historical data needed to write a history of the monument. The monthly and annual operational reports of the Engineer in Charge of Construction and the proceedings of the Joint Commission as well as contracts and correspondence provide a wealth of data on the day-to-day affairs of design and construction of the monument.

Washington, D.C. National Archives and Records Service. Records of the Corps of Engineers. Record Group 77. The General Correspondence file is especially helpful in this group.

Washington, D.C. National Archives and Records Service. Records of the National Park Service. Cartographic Records, 1791-1958. Record Group 79. This collection of drawings, plans, and maps is extremely useful to a history of the monument.

Government Documents

Next to Record Group 42, the following list of government printed documents provides an inexhaustible body of information on the history of the monument from the earliest days to the end of the Corps of Engineer's involvement. Many of the annual and monthly operational reports of the Engineer in Charge of Construction are published here, but in addition, these volumes include detailed accounts of appropriations, names of contractors, opposing views in Congress concerning designs, early debates in Congress dealing with the idea of a monument, and a variety of extremely valuable information. Without these sources, a history of the monument would be difficult.

Ford, Worthington Chauncey, Gaillard Hunt, John C. Fitzpatrick, and Roscoe R. Hill, eds. *Journal of the Continental Congress.* Washington: Government Printing Office, 1904-37. Volumes 24 and 25 deal with the resolution passed by the Continental Congress in 1783 to build a statue to Washington.

U.S. Congress. Senate. Senate Misc. Doc. 17, 46th Cong., 2d sess., 1879.

―――――――. Senate. Senate Misc. Doc. 19, 47th Cong., 1st sess., 1881.

―――――――. Senate. Senate Misc. Doc. 13, 47th Cong., 2d sess., 1882.

―――――――. Senate. Senate Misc. Doc. 22, 48th Cong., 1st sess., 1883.

―――――――. Senate. Senate Exec. Doc. 6, 49th Cong. 1st sess., 1885.

―――――――. Senate. Senate Misc. Doc. 22, 50th Cong., 1st sess., 1887.

―――――――. Senate. Senate Misc. Doc. 142, 50th Cong., 1st sess., 1888.

―――――――. Senate. Senate Report 166, 57th Cong., 1st sess., 1902. Also published as Moore, Charles, ed. *The Improvement of the Park System of the District of Columbia.* Vol. 3. Washington: Government Printing Office, 1902.

―――――――. Senate. Senate Doc. 224, 57th Cong., 2d sess., 1903. Also published as Harvey, Frederick L. *History of the Washington Monument and Washington National Monument Society.* Washington: Government Printing Office, 1903. Harvey was the Society's historian and clerk to the Joint Commission.

U.S. Congress. Senate. Senate Doc. 332, 71st Cong., 3d sess., 1932. Also published as Caemmerer, H. Paul. *Washington: The National Capital.* Washington, D.C.: Government Printing Office, 1932.

―――――――. House. House Report 434, 28th Cong. 1st sess., 1844.

―――――――. House. House Report 94, 33d Cong., 2d sess., 1855. Also published as *Monument to The Memory of Washington.* Washington: A.O.P. Nicholson, Printer, 1855. The published version of this report is in the Rare Book Room of the Library of Congress.

―――――――. House. House Report 48, 42d Cong., 2d sess., 1872.

―――――――. House. House Report 79, 42d Cong., 3d sess., 1873.

_____. House. House Report 485, 43d Cong., 1st sess., 1874.

_____. House. *Washington National Monument: Shall the Unfinished Obelisk stand a Monument of National Disgrace and National Dishonor?* Speech of Hon. John B. Storm, 4 June 1874. Washington: Government Printing Office, 1874.

_____. House. House Misc. Doc. 1, Part 8, 45th Cong., 2d sess., 1877.

_____. House. House Misc. Doc. 7, Part 2, 45th Cong., 3d sess., 1878.

_____. House. House Misc. Doc. 37, 46th Cong., 2d sess., 1880.

_____. House. House Report 1107, 46th Cong., 2d sess., 1880.

_____. House. House Misc. Doc. 8, 48th Cong., 2d sess., 1884.

_____. House. *Improvement of the Base and Grounds of the Washington Monument: Hearing Before The Committee on The Library.* House Report No. 11208. 70th Congress, 1st session.

_____. House. House Doc. 528, 72nd Cong., 2d sess., 1933. Also published as *Improvement of the Washington Monument Grounds, January 19, 1933.* Washington: Government Printing Office, 1934.

_____. *The Dedication of the Washington National Monument with the Orations by Hon. Robert C. Winthrop and Hon. John W. Daniel.* 21 February 1885. Washington: Government Printing Office, 1885.

_____. *The Debates and Proceedings in the Congress of the United States with an Appendix containing Important State Papers and Public Documents, and all The Laws of a Public Nature; with a Copious Index.* Washington: Gales & Seaton, 1851. The issues for the years 1789-1824 bear the title *Annals of Congress.* The later ones bear the title *Register of Debates In Congress.* These documents reveal the debates that went on in Congress from 1789 to 1833 concerning the type of monument that should be built to memorialize Washington and the adequacy of an appropriation for this purpose.

U.S. War Department. Chief of Engineers. *Annual Reports of the Chief of Engineers, U.S. Army.* Fiscal Years 1889 to 1925. Washington: Government Printing Office, 1889-1925. These volumes contain the annual reports of the Officer in Charge of Public Buildings and Grounds to the Chief of Engineers after the Joint Commission was dissolved by Congress. There is much valuable information on the elevator, grounds, and other aspects of the monument's operation during the years following its completion.

_____. Chief of Engineers. *Annual Reports of the Director of Public Buildings and Public Parks of the National Capital.* 1926 to

1932. Washington: Government Printing Office, 1926-32. These documents contain the annual reports of the monument by the Director of Public Buildings and Public Parks of the National Capital from the time this office was established until the monument was transferred to the custodianship of the National Park Service.

Printed Sources

American Medical Association. *Circular Issued by Committee Appointed to Solicit Funds for a Stone In the Washington Monument.* Lancaster, Pa.: American Medical Association, 7 February 1853.

Gedney, C.D. *Sketches of Engraved Stone Tablets Contributed to the Washington National Monument.* Privately published: 17 February 1880. About half of the stones drawn in this work were from those stones already in the monument and the rest were drawn from those still remaining in the lapidarium. This copy is in the Rare Book Room of the Library of Congress.

Gedney, C.D. *Sketches of Engraved Stone Tablets Contributed to the Washington National Monument.* Privately published: 17 February 1880. About half of the stones drawn in this work were from those stones already in the monument and the rest were drawn from those still remaining in the lapidarium. This copy is in the Rare Book Room of the Library of Congress.

Nevins, Allen, ed. *The Diary of a President, 1845-1849.* New York: Longmanns, Green and Co., 1929. In his diary President Polk describes the laying of the cornerstone in great detail.

Poore, Ben Perley. *Perley's Reminiscences of Sixty Years In the National Metropolis.* 2 vols. Philadelphia: Hubbard Brothers, Pub., 1886. Volume 2 concerns the construction history of the monument as the author remembers it.

Roose's Companion and Guide to Washington and Vicinity. Washington: Gibson Brothers, Printers, 1887.

The Washington National Monument: Views of the Early Patriots Regarding it; Reason Why It Should Remain On Its Present Site; Objects and Uses of Such Structures; An Appeal to the People and Their Representatives. Washington: Washington National Monument Society, 1871. A copy may be found in the Rare Book Room of the Library of Congress.

Roose's Companion and Guide to Washington and Vicinity. Washington: Gibson Brothers, Printers, 1887.

The Washington National Monument: Views of the Early Patriots Regarding it; Reason Why It Should Remain On Its Present Site; Objects and Uses of Such Structures; An Appeal to the People and Their

Representatives. Washington: Washington National Monument Society, 1871. A copy may be found in the Rare Book Room of the Library of Congress.

van Brunt, Henry. *The American Art Review*. 1880. One of the most critical reviews of the Mills and the modified designs of the monument as well as a critical survey of some of the more prominent plans offered in their place by a well-known critic of the period.

Wershampel, John F. *The Pope's Strategem: Rome to America: An Address to the Protestants of the United States Against Placing the Pope's Block of Marble in the Washington Monument*. Baltimore: [1852]. A copy of this publication is in the Rare Book Room of the Library of Congress.

Williams, Charles Richard. *The Life of Rutherford Birchard Hayes: Nineteenth President of the United States*. 2 vols. Boston: Houghton, Mifflin Co., 1914. Volume 2 contains President Hayes's views concerning the monument and Casey's role.

Secondary Works

Bryan, Wilhelemus Bogart. *A History of the National Capital: From Its Foundation Through the Period of the Adoption of the Organic Act*. 2 vols. New York: The MacMillan Co., 1916. Volume 2 deals with the monument.

Carrington, Henry B. *The Obelisk and Its Voices or, The Inner Facings of the Washington Monument, With their Lessons*. Boston: Lee and Shepard, Publisher, 1887.

Cooling, Benjamin Franklin. *Symbol, Sword, and Shield*. Hampden, Conn.: Archon Books, 1975.

Cowdrey, Albert E. *A City for the Nation: The Army Engineers and the Building of Washington, D.C., 1790-1967*. Washington: Office of the Chief of Engineers, 1978.

Ellis, John B., Dr. *The Sights and Secrets of the National Capital: A Work Descriptive of Washington City In All Its Various Phases*. New York: United States Publishing Company, 1869.

Ewing, Charles. *Yesterday's Washington, D.C.* Miami, Florida: E.A. Seemann Publishing, Inc., 1976.

Gallagher, H.M. Pierce. *Robert Mills: Architect of The Washington Monument, 1781-1855*. New York: Columbia University Press, 1935. Reprinted by AMS Press, New York, 1966.

Green, Constance. McLaughlin. *Washington Village and Capital, 1800-1887*. Volume I. Princeton: Princeton University Press, 1962.

_____. *Washington, Capital City, 1879-1950*. Volume II. Princeton University Press, 1963.

Griffith, J.E. *History of the Washington Monument.* Holyoke, Mass.: J. Eveleth Griffith, Printer, 1885.

Gutheim, Frederick. *Worthy of the Nation: The History of Planning for the National Capital.* Washington: Smithsonian Institution, 1977.

Hamlin, Talbot. *Greek Revival Architecture in America: Being an Account of Important Trends in American Architecture and American Life Prior to the War Between the States.* New York: Dover Publications, Inc., 1944.

Moore, Charles. *Washington Past and Present.* New York: The Century Co., 1929. Moore was one of the most active supporters of the McMillan Plan.

Moore, Joseph West. *Picturesque Washington: Pen and Pencil Sketches.* Providence: J. A. and R.A. Reid, 1887.

Murdock, Myrtle Cheney. *Your Memorials In Washington.* Washington: Monumental Press, Inc., 1952.

Nicolay, Helen. *Our Capital on the Potomac.* New York: The Century Co., 1924.

Proctor, John Clagett, ed. *Washington Past and Present: A History.* 4 vols. New York: Lewis Historical Publishing Company, Inc., 1930. Volume 2 talks of the monument.

Reps, John W. *Monumental Washington: The Planning and Development of the Capital Center.* Princeton: Princeton University Press, 1967.

Shackleton, Robert. *The Book of Washington.* Philadelphia: The Penn Publishing Company, 1923.

The Washington Monument. Washington: The Society of American Military Engineers, 1923.

Walton, William. *The Evidence of Washington.* Washington: Harper and Row, 1966.

Writers Program of the Work Projects Administration for the District of Columbia, comp. *Washington, D.C.: A Guide to The Nation's Capital.* Sponsored by George Washington University. New York: Hastings House, 1942.

Periodicals

Avery, Henry O. "The Washington Monument." *American Architect and Building News.* Vol. 26 (13 December 1884). Also see the following issues of this periodical on the monument: Vol. 8 (10 July 1880), Vol. 8 (11 September 1880), and Vol. 16 (9 August 1884). This magazine was a strong critic of the monument's modified design.

Bing, Richard. "George Washington's Monument." *Constructor.* Vol. 58 (December 1976): 18-25.

Ditzell, Paul. "How They Built the Washington Monument." *The Ameri-*

can *Legion Magazine,* February 1968, 25ff.
Frank Leslie's Illustrated, 1 February 1862. This issue contains a wood engraving of the scene around the monument during the Civil War.
"George Washington's Monument." *American Heritage.* Vol. 20 (December 1968): 68-73.
Gutheim, Frederick. "Who Designed the Washington Monument? An address read before the annual meeting of the Society of Architectural Historians, Washington, D.C., January 28, 1951." *Journal of the American Institute of Architects.* Vol. 15 (1951).
Harpers Weekly, 29 November 1884, 789-90.
Huxtable, Ada Louise. "The Washington Monument, 1836-1884." *Progressive Architecture.* Vol. 38 (August 1957): 141-44.
Parkill, S.M. "Washington National Monument." *Compressed Air Magazine,* September 1957, 266-69.
"Robert Mills and The Washington Monument in Baltimore." *The Maryland Historical Magazine.* Vol. 34 (June 1939): 144-60.
Weart, D.L. "Erection of the Washington Monument." *The Military Engineer.* Vol. 15 (March-April 1932): 99-102.

Newspapers

The National Intelligencer. Washington, D.C. 24 September 1833; 15 September 1848; and 8 March 1854.
The New York Herald. 1 January 1871.
The New York Tribune. 1 July 1875.
The Washington Post. 22 November 1894.

Biographical Works

Abbott, Henry L., ed. "Memoirs of Thomas Lincoln Casey, 1831-1896." *National Academy of Sciences, Biographical Memoirs.* 1902. Vol. 4. pp. 125-34.
Centennial of the United States Military Academy at West Point, New York 1802-1901. Washington: 1904. Revised edition. New York: Greenwood Press, 1969. pp. 852-55.
Johnson, Allen and Dumas Malone, eds., *Dictionary of American Biography.* New York: Charles Scribner's Sons, 1964.

INDEX

Accidents, 101
Adams, John Quincy, 9
Alston, Willis, 4
American Party, see Know-Nothing Party
American Revolution, 1
Apex, see Pyramidion
Appropriations, 49, 76-77, 78, 88, 89, 101, 108, 109
   decline, 93
   denied, 26, 30
   for dedication, 86
   for foundation, 36, 42, 49, 54, 56, 73, 78
   for mausoleum, 5
   for McMillan Plan, 112
   for memorial stones, 93
   for opening of Monument, 99
   from states and territories, 30
   opposition to, 37
   recommended, 33, 97
   to resume construction, 37
   to Society, 26
Arthur, Chester A., President, 82, 87

Babcock Lake, 94, 95, 110
Babylonian Architecture, 13
Barnard, Brevet Major General John G., 36
Bell, M. E., 82
Bingham, Colonel Theodore A., 102, 108
Blacksmith Shop, 59, 60, 86
Blake, John, 40-41
Board of Engineers for Fortifications, 36-37
Boiler house, 89-90
Brent, John Carroll, 32
Briggs, John A. (marble contractor), 63, 64
Briggs, Samuel, 26
Bronze Plaque, 104-105
Buchanan, President James, 5-6
Building Committee (Joint Committee, 1878), 44-45, 54, 66, 67, 69, 70, 80, 93, 95, 110
   members, 44
Building Committee (Society, 1848), 16, 17, 18, 19, 20, 92, 109
   See also Thomas Carbery
Burnham, Daniel H., 111

Capstone, see Pyramidion
Carbery, Thomas, 19, 21
Casey, Lieutenant Colonel Thomas Lincoln, 42-43, 44, 54, 57-58, 87, 97, 103, 104, 105, 106, 109, 114
   begins work on foundation, 59-67
   completes the Monument, 89-97
   plans for obelisk, 73-77
   plans for superstructure, 56-58
   pyramidion, 78-85
   relations with Corcoran, 45
   modifications of Monument, 47-49
   relations with Building Committee, 44-45
   relations with Society, 45-46
   solves foundation problem, 47-49
Casey, Brevet Major General Silas, 42
Chipman, Norton P., 32, 36
Civil War, 25, 28, 114
   effect on contributions, 23, 28
Claiborne, William, 4
Clark, Edward, 38, 45, 57, 58, 82
Clay, Henry, 9
Congress, 16, 23, 46, 52, 53, 94-95, 97, 108
   failure to act, 14, 36, 96
   House Committee on Public Buildings and Grounds, 14
   McMillan Plan, 112
   Senate Committee on Public Buildings and Grounds, 103
   special commission for dedication, 86
   Casey's plan for completing Monument, 94-95
   select committee on foundation, 32, 33, 34-36, 37
   See also Appropriations
   See also Building Committee
Congressional Resolutions, 14
   See also Equestrian statue
Continental Congress, 1, 2, 4
Contractors, 17, 112
   problems, 62, 64, 76, 90
   See also individual contractors
Contributions, 20, 27, 31-32
   Ives' role, 28
   problems, 9, 14, 21, 23, 25, 26, 27, 28
   use of agents, 9

Corcoran, William W., 38, 44, 45-46, 57, 58, 82, 87, 103
Cornerstone, 19, 76, 82
Corps of Engineers, 39, 41, 46, 62, 104, 105, 106, 107, 113, 114
    custody of Monument, 97
    Marshall Report, 33-34, 36
Craighill, Colonel Williams P., 58
Cranch, Judge William, 8

Dallas, George W., 9
Davis, Captain George W., 42, 43, 44, 58, 62, 64, 76, 84, 125 fn. 65
Deaths, 102
Dedication, 86-87
Delays, 6, 17, 59, 62, 63, 67-68, 69 76, 81, 103
Designs, *see* Equestrian statue, Mills Design, Story Plan
Director of Public Buildings and Public Parks of the National Capital, *see* Office of Public Buildings and Grounds
Doorways, 78, 90-91, 94
Dougherty, William, 17, 18, 20
    relations with Know-Nothings, 26
Duane, Lieutenant Colonel James C., 39

Early, William (blue stone contractor), 17
Edwards, A. L., 44
Egyptian Architecture, 9, 11, 13, 23, 55, 90, 94
Elevator, 61, 73-74, 76, 77, 89-90, 94, 99, 102
    electric system, 107-108, 130 fn. 43
    heating system, 102
    inspections, 106, 107, 109
    problems, 106-107
    See also Otis Brothers and Company
Ellsworth, Oliver, 1
Embankment, 70
Emery, Mathew G., 19
Equestrian Statue
    Resolution of 1783, 1, 2, 3, 4, 5, 6
    Resolution of 1799, 3, 6
    Resolution of 1803, 5
Expenses, 44, 59, 76, 89, 97, 99, 100, 108, 113
Fillmore, President Millard, 9
Floor, 92
Florentine Gothic Architecture, 52
Floyd, John (Secretary of War), 27

Force, Peter, 8
Foundation
    Casey's plan, 54-56
    criticism, 47
    inspections, 19, 27, 33
    See also Ives Report
    See also Kingman Report
    See also Marshall Report
Friebus, Gustav, 44
Frishmuth, William, 81
Fund Raising, *see* Contributions

Gallatin, Albert, 9
Gillette, Major Douglas H., 113
Gilmore, Lieutenant Colonel Quincy A., 39
Grant, Lieutenant Colonel Ulysses S. III, 112
Grant, President Ulysses S., 38
Greek Architecture, 11, 13
Greek Revival Architecture, 4, 11, 13-14, 17
Green, Bernard Richardson, 43-44, 58, 78-80, 84, 105-106
Greenough, Horatio, 6, 15

Hamlin, Talbot, 13-14
Harper, Robert Goodloe, 4
Hayes, President Rutherford B., 41, 46, 57, 58, 76
Heating System, 102
Hepburn, David, 18
Hill, James G., 38, 58
Houdon, Jean, 6
Huger, Benjamin, 5
Humphreys, Major General Andrew P., 32, 33, 38, 41, 42, 52, 58
    select committee on foundation, 32, 33
Huxtable, Ada Louise
    on Mills design, 49-52

Interior Walls, problems with condensation, 92, 105-106
Ives, Lieutenant Joseph C., 27-28
Ives Report (1859), 28, 33, 40-41

J. B. White and Brothers (Portland cement contractors), 62
Jackson, President Andrew, 8
Johnson, President Andrew, 30

Joint Commission on the Construction of the Washington National Monument, 38, 41, 44, 46, 58, 63, 76, 93, 94, 95, 96, 97, 103, 105, 109, 111
   appointed, 37
   dedication, 86
   dissolved, 97
   Kingman report, 40-42
   Story Plan, 52-53
   supports Casey, 49, 59, 61, 74, 80, 91, 103, 104

Kingman, Lieutenant Dan C., 39
Kingman Report, 39-42, 47
Know-Nothing Party, 25-27, 46, 74
   See also Pope's Stone
Kurtz, Lieutenant Colonel John D., 39

L'Enfant, Pierre Charles, 2, 15, 16, 111
Labor Force, 18, 59, 66
   granite cutters, 66-67
   marble cutters, 66
   problems, 62, 67, 81
   recruiting, 59, 65
   reorganization, 73
   skilled workers, 65
   stonecutters, 66, 67
   wages, 18, 64, 65, 66, 67
Lapidarium, 22, 59, 93
Latrobe, Benjamin, 1, 9, 11
Lee Marble Company, 63-64, 77
Lee, Arthur, 1
Lee, Henry, 3, 4
Lighting System, 78, 89, 92, 102
Lightning, 90, 91-92

Machinery, 60
Macon, Nathaniel, 4
Madison, Dolley, 19
Madison, James, 8
Mall, 15, 16, 87, 111, 112
Marble Lodge, 104, 109-110
Marsh, George Perkins, 55-56, 58, 78, 80, 85
   work with Casey, 56, 57
Marshall, John, 2, 8
Marshall, Lieutenant William Louis, 33
   See also Marshall Report, 33
Marshall Report
   first report, 33-34
   second report, 34, 36, 40-41
Massachusetts Marble Company, 77
Mausoleum, 4-6

May, Congressman Henry, 26, 27
McKim, Charles F., 111
McLaughlin, P. H., 67, 84
McMillan Plan, 110, 111-112
McMillan, Sen. James, 111
Mead, Larkin G., 94
Meigs, General Montgomery C., 57-58
Memorial Stones, 21-22, 73, 78, 89, 92, 104
   Alabama, 21
   American Medical Association, 21
   criticism of, 93
   Masons, 93
   Odd-Fellows, 93
   Sons of Temperance, 93
   See also Lapidarium
Mifflin, Thomas, 1
Mills, Robert, 9, 17, 18, 19, 20, 23
   See also Mills Design
Mills Design, 9-15, 21, 27, 53, 57, 58, 90, 93-94, 97, 98, 111
   criticism, 13-14, 34, 36, 37-38, 46, 47, 49-52, 57, 58, 93, 97
Moore, Charles, 98

National Capitol Park and Planning Commission, 112
National Park Service, 105, 114
Navarre, B. F., 44
Newton, John, 82
Nicholas, John, 4
Nott, Abraham, 4

Obelisk Water Proofing Company, 106
Office of Public Buildings and Grounds, custody of, 97, 99, 102, 103, 104, 106, 108, 109, 110, 111, 112
   See also Bingham
   See also Wilson
Olmstead, Frederick Law, Jr., 98, 111, 113
Otis Brothers and Company, 74, 90, 107

Peale, Charles, 2
Phoenix Iron Company, 74
Polk, President James K., 9, 16, 19, 20
Poore, Ben Perley, 86
Pope's Stone, 25-26
Proctor, Redfield (Secretary of War), 105
Public Buildings and Parks of the National Capitol, 106

Pyramidion, 77, 78-85, 89, 91-92, 102
   apex, 81-84, 91
   shutters, 85
   windows, 85
   capstone, 81-82

Quarries, 63, 76, 77
   Baltimore County, MD, 62, 63
   Potomac Valley, 19
   Sheffield, MA, 62, 63
   Westchester County, NY, 17

Reception Room, 102

Safety, 19, 60, 67, 89, 102-103, 107
   See also lightning
   See also Ives Report
Seaton, William W., 8
Select Committee, 34
Sherman, Senator, 87
Sisson, Hugh (marble contractor), 63, 64, 77, 91
Site, selection of, 14, 15-16
Smith, Samuel H., 8
Society, See Washington National Monument Society
Spofford, Mr., 57
St. Gaudens, Augustus, 111
Stairs, 73, 75-76, 77, 89
Stone-dressing, change in industry, 17
Stonecutters Shed, 59-60
Story Plan, 52-54
Story, William Wetmore, 52
Strikes, see Contractors, problems
Stuart, Charles, 6
Stuart, Fred E., 47
Suicides, 102
Symington, Thomas (marble contractor), 17, 18, 19

Taylor, Zachary, 9
Terrace, 33, 70, 78, 90, 95, 97, 110-111
Thomas, Charles, 1
Thomas, George M., 99
Toner, Dr. Joseph M., 76
Tower, Brevet Major General John G., 36
Towers, John T., 25

van Brunt, Henry, 13, 52
Van Ness, John P., 8
Vandalism, 25, 60, 95-96, 103-104
Vanderlyn, John, 6

Victorian Architecture, 40, 49-52
Visitors, 85, 96-97, 100-104, 107, 108, 109
   attendance, 90, 100
   comfort of, 102
   special requests to use Monument, 101-102

War Department, 45, 96, 97, 107, 109
   custody of Monument, 95, 96
War of 1812, 5
Washington Centennial, 6, 32, 36
Washington, DC, 1, 2, 15, 111
   See also Mall
Washington, George, 1, 16, 39, 86, 87, 98
   centennial of birth, 6, 32, 37
   portraits and statues, 1, 2, 6, 94
   See also Washington Centennial
Washington, John A., 6
Washington, Martha, 3
Washington Monument
   closings, 101
   criticism of, 29, 97-98
   hours of operation, 99, 100
   maintenance, 108, 109, 111
   opening of, 97, 99
   operating costs, 99, 100
   praise of, 97, 98
   requests to use the Monument, 100, 101
   staff, 99, 100, 103
   visitors hours, 101, 103
   workday, 99
Washington National Monument Society, 7, 13, 17, 23, 27, 30, 37, 38, 53, 57, 97, 107, 108, 109
   advises Joint Commission on Story Plln, 52-53
   bronze plaque, 104, 105
   control of, 26-27
   criticism of, 9
   expenses, 17, 20, 21, 97
   formation, 7-9
   fund raising, 9
   incorporation, 27
   internal affairs, 23, 25
   Kingman Report, 40-42
   members, 8
   memorial stones, 21-22, 105
   plans for dedication, 86
   records, 46, 73, 109
   relations with Congress, 25, 32, 46

Story Plan, 54
  transfer of Monument, 38
 See also Building Committee
 See also Watterston
Watterston, George, 7-8, 14
Webster, Daniel, 9
William M. Poindexter and Company
  (architects), 110
Wilson, Colonel John M., 97, 99, 102,
  103, 104, 107, 109, 110
Winthrop, Congressman Robert C.,
  19, 53, 56, 57, 58
Work Force, *see* Labor Force
Wright, Brevet Major General Horatio
  G., 36, 58

www.ingramcontent.com/pod-product-compliance
Lightning Source LLC
Chambersburg PA
CBHW071724090426
42738CB00009B/1870